ACTIVE  PARENTING
First Five Years™

Parent's Guide

Written by
Michael H. Popkin, PhD

Contributing Authors:
Amanda Sheffield Morris, PhD, IMH-E®
Ruth Slocum, LCSW, IMH-E®
Laura Hubbs-Tait, PhD

Photography by Melody Popkin and TT Coles

ISBN 1-59723-343-9
978-1-59723-343-9

Dedications

This program is dedicated to the most important family
in the world to your children: yours.

With appreciation to the George Kaiser Family Foundation

TABLE OF CONTENTS

CHAPTER 1: You and Your Child

Parents have a special job. 7
Children are special people! 8
Activity: One Strength 11
Ages and Stages Chart 21
Your Child's Nature (Temperament) 23
Parenting Styles 24
The Power of Choice 27
Choices Worksheet 29
Building a Bond with Your Child 30
Paying Attention to Feelings 32
Every Day, a Little Play 33
Brain-Building Activity: Follow the Lead 35
Playing to Learn Chart 36
Taking Care of Yourself. 38
Self-Care Chart 39
Mindfulness: An Introduction 40
Mindful Moment: The Mind Jar 41
Home Activities 43

CHAPTER 2: Preventing Problems

Problems are a part of life 45
Your Child's Beautiful Brain 45
Brain-Building Activity: Freeze Dance. 48
Mindful Moment: Many Ways to Breathe 49
Keeping Your Child Safe and Sound 51
Safe Home Checklist. 54
Playing Safe Checklist 57
Finding Good Childcare 58
Teaching your child is important 60
Getting Discipline "Just Right" 61
Listening to What Your Child Needs 62
Getting Your Child to Come When You Call 62
The Beauty of a Good Rule. 65
Making Rules Worksheet 68
Discipline Skill: The When-Then Rule 69
When-Then Rule Worksheet 70
Discipline Skills: The ACT Method 71

ACT Method Worksheet 75
Building the Bond: Routines 76
Routines Worksheet 77
The Importance of Sleep 80
Building the Bond: Hugs, Kisses, and 3 Little Words 80
"I Love You" Worksheet 81
Taking Care of Yourself Worksheet 82
Home Activities 83

CHAPTER 3: Encouraging Positive Behavior

Temperament and Discipline 85
Temperament Worksheet 89
Discipline Skill: Choices and Consequences 90
Choices and Consequences Worksheet 95
Brain-Building Activity: Panda and Frog 96
Tantrums 100
Tantrums Worksheet 105
Mindful Moment: Loving Kindness 106
Encouraging Your Child 107
Encouragement Worksheet 111
You need encouragement, too! 112
Where You Can Go for Help 113
Home Activities 115

CHAPTER 4: Preparing for School Success

Watering Your Child's Beautiful Brain 117
Six Smart Things Parents Can Do to
Help Their Child Get Ready for School 118
Smart Thing #1: Encourage play 118
Brain-Building Activity: Working Memory 121
Smart Thing #2: Encourage learning 123
Smart Thing #3: Read and talk with your child 126
Smart Thing #4: Limit screen time 130
Smart Thing #5: Teach social skills 132
Emotional Intelligence 133
Video Practice: Identifying and Responding to Feelings 135
Smart Thing #6: Stimulate independence 138
The B.E.S.T. Way to Teach Skills 140
Mindful Moment: Mindful Parenting 142
Your child needs you 143
Final Thoughts 143

CHAPTER 1 You and Your Child

Parents have a special job.

If you are a parent you have an important job. And since raising children usually involves other caregivers as well, when we say "parent" in this book, we also mean all those you trust with your child's care, too. Your job as a parent or other caregiver is to protect your child. You also have a job to teach your child. Your child cannot survive or be his best by himself. He needs your help.

A parent's number one job is to protect. That means making sure your kids…

- Eat healthy food.

- Go to the doctor for check-ups and immunizations (shots that protect).

- Have safe places to play.

- Are always supervised by a responsible adult (never left alone anywhere—especially a car!).

- Are safe from abuse or neglect.

So, keeping your child safe and healthy is your first job, and we will talk much more about how to do this in Chapter 2. But there is more: How will your child grow up? Will she help others? Will she hurt others? Will she live a good life? Your job as a parent is special. You can help your child be a responsible person who can take care of herself and others when she grows up. In other words, will your child thrive?

THE PURPOSE OF PARENTING
To protect and prepare our children
to survive and thrive
in the kind of society in which they will live.

The ideas in this book will help you. Remember, you are the parent. You will decide how to guide your child. Listen to your heart and your mind. We hope you will also use the ideas in this book.

Most parents find that like most jobs, parenting is part joy and part chore. Parts of it are a pleasure to do and parts of it are just things that have to be done to get the job done right. Keeping a positive attitude can help. Know that the time you spend on both the joys and the chores will pay off for your lifetime, your child's lifetime, and for lifetimes to come.

Remember that you don't have to do it all by yourself. Children don't have to learn everything from their parents. They can also learn from teachers, grandparents, aunts and uncles, friends, and other caregivers. As you think about parenting, do not worry about your mistakes. All parents make mistakes. The best thing you can do is learn from them. Do not blame yourself when you make a mistake. Think about what you can do better the next time. This will make you a better parent for your child.

Children are special people!

We all know that children are different from adults because:

- They are smaller.
- They do not know as much as adults.
- They cannot talk like adults.

Children are also different because:

- They think differently.
- They do not always know what is dangerous.
- They need to play (it is how they learn).
- They need adults to help them grow up well.

Children are the same as adults in one important way:

- They have the same feelings: happiness, sadness, anger, and many others.

Your child will change a lot in the first five years of her life. These changes happen in stages. If you understand these stages, you will understand your child better. This guide will explain the changes during each year: birth, age 1, age 2, age 3, and age 4. This is why we call it *Active Parenting: First Five Years*. We have given each of the five stages a name:

Birth to 1 - The "Baby"

Age 1 - The Explorer

Age 2 - The Boss

Age 3 - The Pal

Age 4 - The Adventurer

Children are different at each stage, and at each stage they grow, develop, and learn. In fact, they cannot move on to the next stage until they learn certain things. Your job is to help your child learn these things and grow. You want her to learn to grow without hurting herself, other people, or anything else.

But remember, it isn't a race. All children go through these stages in order, but they go through at different speeds. If you push to make them go faster, you are more likely to cause problems than to help them. Support them, but don't rush them.

Age-Appropriate Behavior

The idea behind these ages and stages is that certain behavior is normal or appropriate at certain ages and not at others. Here are four reasons why it is helpful to know what is normal behavior at different stages:

1. **It helps you understand your child's job at different ages.** Being aware of ages and stages helps you understand that sometimes when you think your child is misbehaving, he may really just be trying to do his job. For example, when your

two-year-old "Boss" tells you, "No, I don't want to!" You don't have to take it personally because you know he is just doing his job of testing his power… and maybe your patience, too.

2. **It helps you not expect too much from your child too soon.** On page 21 you'll see a chart of ages and some of the milestones that children can reach at these ages. For example, children are usually ready to be potty trained between ages two to three. You'll notice that this skill crosses two years because each child is different. Some children are ready to be potty trained at age two. Others need to develop more muscle control and aren't ready until age three. So don't think of these ages as absolute.

3. **It helps you prevent serious problems.** Once you know the kinds of things your child will do at his age, you can anticipate problems. For example, once you know that one-year-olds like to explore, you will expect your one-year-old to explore anything you leave on the floor, such as marbles. Since he might put them in his mouth and choke on them, you will now know to keep those marbles off the floor. And remember that babies like to put things in their mouths, too, and they will start exploring as soon as they can scoot or crawl.

4. **It helps you provide safe ways for your child to do her job and be ready to move on to the next stage.** While you are trying not to expect too much from your child and you're trying to prevent problems, you still want to provide safe and acceptable ways for your child to do her job. Remember that that's how she learns.

Children with Special Needs

Some children have special needs that require extra help going through these stages of development. If you notice that your child is not going through these stages like other children his age, ask your pediatrician about it. She can help you decide if your child needs extra help, and if so, where to get it.

✎ ✎ ✎ Activity: One Strength ✎ ✎ ✎

In the blanks below, write the name of each of your children and everyone else who lives in your home, including yourself. Then write one strength that you see in each person that you listed.

NAME	ONE STRENGTH
_____	_____
_____	_____
_____	_____
_____	_____
_____	_____
_____	_____
_____	_____
_____	_____

The Ages and Stages Song

Birth–1: The Baby

When I arrived, I gave a cry
To tell the world, "I'm here!"
I sure was cute in my birthday suit
And my parents held me dear.

They hugged me and kissed me
And sang me sweet songs.
They kept me close and warm as toast
And I felt that I belonged

I watched and I heard every single word,
My brain taking it all in.
I cried and they soothed;
they smiled and I cooed.
Life sure was sweet back then.

Chorus

Ages and stages, one at a time;
Help me move through them, help me
grow fine.
Ages and stages, at my own pace;
No need to rush me, this isn't a race.

Age 1: The Explorer

When I was one, the world was fun:
My empire to explore.
I'd dart and dash and sometimes crash,
And my bottom would hit the floor.

The world was new, and I was too.
I had to touch each thing.
It went to my mouth to figure it out
Then I'd throw it aside with a fling.

I went exploring—it never was boring.
My motto was "Let's check it out."

My mind and my body were growing like
crazy:
A handful, without a doubt.

Age 2: The Boss

When I was two, the world I knew
Was always mine to rule.
I used my powers (and smashed some
towers)
And demanded that you be cool.

Now in command, I did not understand
That I couldn't have my own way.
I said, "Do as you're told, 'cause I'm big
and I'm bold,
And my tantrums can ruin your day."

At times a delight, you'd love me in spite
Of how often I made you say "no."
My job was to test and give you no rest.
No wonder your energy was low.

Age 3: The Pal

When I was three, I'd beg and plead
To go outside and play.
I jumped on a swing and a big sliding thing
And laughed with my buddies all day.

Although I was known to play on my own,
I was ready to make some new friends.
My mind worked so fast, so much language
at last!
That my questions seemed never to end.

Sometimes not too sure, I felt insecure
But was usually ready to learn.
I loved a good book. You read and I looked,
Practiced sharing and taking my turn.

12

Age 4: The Adventurer

When I was four I wanted more
Adventure, so I took to the sea.
I sailed far and wide in my tub on the tide:
Ducky and Teddy and me.

No limitation to my imagination,
Playing pretend was so cool.
I could also be wild, a challenging child
Testing the limits and rules.

It's not I was bad, but the pleasure I had
In trying so many new things
Left me cranky and tired and sometimes
just wired
From growing my roots and my wings.

Chorus:

Ages and stages, one at a time;
Help me move through them, help me
grow fine.
Ages and stages, tend me with care.
Love me forever and joy we will share.

Age Birth to 1 - The Baby

Your baby comes into the world all fresh and new. It's so exciting! It's so amazing! It's so scary. Why? Because you realize that this little being depends on you (and those you trust) for her very survival. You are responsible for her in a way you may have never been before. And it is wise to feel a little scared at first.

But you already know a lot about the job, and you will learn the rest. Pretty soon you will be so busy taking care of your baby that you won't feel scared anymore… except for the healthy fear that all parents have for their children. Don't let go of that. It reminds you to watch out for anything that might hurt your child.

Your baby may seem helpless when she is born, but she actually has some pretty good instincts. For example, she already knows how to breathe, suck, and poop. By the time she is one year old, chances are she will already know how to crawl, stand, walk and maybe even say a few words. In fact she will grow so fast that if you don't see her all day you may notice when you get home that she has already changed a little bit!

Even though your baby sleeps a lot, she is a very active learner. Whatever you give, whether it's food, love, smiles, or words, she will soak it up. But your baby does a lot more than that. Her tiny little brain is growing like crazy, making sense of all those sights, sounds, tastes, and feelings, even when she is just lying on her back staring at the ceiling. So, don't try to keep her busy all of the time. Let her have time to do the amazing brain-work we do not yet fully understand.

Here are some things to remember:

- Your baby depends on you for survival. It is up to you to provide food, clothing, shelter, and everything else she needs to be safe and healthy. She cannot do these things for herself. She is helpless to survive and thrive on her own. Be sure to read the Infant Safety information on page 53.

- Your baby also needs love and nurturing from you. She will respond well to hugs, kisses, smiles, sweet talk, singing, reading, and other forms of nurture. Without these things, she may survive, but she will not thrive.

- Whenever you drive with your baby in the car, she must be in a safety seat. There are rules about safety seats that you need to be aware of and follow closely. Be sure to read the information about safety seats on page 52.

- Everything is new to a baby. She uses her five senses to take it all in: watching, listening, smelling, tasting, cooing, reaching, touching. Pay attention to what your baby is interested in. She is showing you what she is ready to learn about!

- Crying is a baby's way of saying, "Pay attention!" She is telling you that she needs something. So it is important that you go to her and try to figure out what the cry means. Babies whose cries are attended tend to cry less over time. They learn to trust that you'll be there when they need you.

- Give your baby lots of time and attention. Get down on her level, look into her eyes, and show her that you are paying attention. Respond when she coos, babbles, talks, or smiles.

- Babies love gentle movement like walking, rocking, and dancing. Often it has a calming effect on them, especially combined with soft talking or singing.

- Talk to your baby. Sing and play games. She will enjoy stories, rhymes, and gentle games like peek-a-boo. A baby's growing brain takes in every word and sound, helping to develop early language skills. Plus, the sound of your voice will soothe your baby.

Age 1: The "Explorer"

Your one-year-old is really starting to learn about the world in this stage. He is seeing, hearing, touching, tasting, and smelling more every day. This is how he learns. Exploring things will help him develop his mind and learn how things work. There is also one huge difference you will notice.

Your child is learning to walk. He can now explore places that were beyond his world a few months ago. He runs everywhere. He touches and tastes everything. This is great for his mind, but it can be dangerous. Your job is to make sure he learns about the world in a safe way.

Here are some things to remember:

- Get down on the floor and see your house as your child sees it. What can she reach? What can hurt her? Put away things that could break or fall on her or anything that could be harmful, such as household cleaners. There are more of these tips in the Safe Home Checklist on page 54.

- Make a safe place where your one-year-old can play. You cannot play with your child every minute, so she needs to have a place to move and play by herself. Find a place where she can play without getting hurt or breaking something. Put up a safety gate to keep her in this safe place. There are more of these tips in the Playing Safe Checklist on page 57.

- Always buckle your child into a safety seat while in the car. It is the law in all fifty states. Be a good role model and wear a seatbelt, too.

- Never leave your child alone. It is not safe. When you are at home but your child is out of your sight or hearing range, check on her a lot. If you want to take a nap or a shower, put her in a safety-approved crib or playpen. When you are away from home with your child, never leave her alone, especially in a car.

- Make sure the toys your child plays with are safe for one-year-olds. At this stage, your child likes to put things in her mouth. So make sure that what she plays with is too big to go in her mouth and choke her. There is a list of safe toys for your one-year-old in the Playing to Learn Chart on page 36.

- All children are curious. They want to know about everything. So give your child things she can learn with. Bring home a big cardboard box that she can climb in (but make sure there are no staples). One-year-olds also love to play with small plastic tubs and lids, pots and pans, and picture books. These things can keep them busy and happy for a long time.

- You can begin to make rules for your child at this stage, but do not expect her to be able to follow them all the time. Sometimes she will forget that she should not throw toys or stand on a rocking chair. A one-year-old child forgets quickly. She is still learning to remember things. Stay calm and remind your child of how to act safely. You may need to take her away from dangerous places.

■ Your child may try acting in hurtful ways. She may even try biting or kicking. When this happens, do not get angry or yell. Instead, look her in the eye and say, "No biting!" or "No kicking!" in a firm voice. If you get angry or start yelling, she may keep doing it to see if you will get mad again. We will learn more about discipline in Chapters 2 and 3.

Age 2: The Boss

Your two-year-old is learning about his abilities. He is learning how to get things done and how to make things happen, and that feels powerful. But he is also learning that he cannot always have things his way. Your child needs to learn to use his power in useful ways.

He will learn by testing you. He may do things he knows are wrong to make you angry. He wants to test you to see if you mean what you say. That's why it is your job to say "no" sometimes. You will need to make the rules.

When you make rules for your two-year-old, he will learn that "no" is a powerful word. Then he will try to use it on you! When this happens, you need to stay calm. Your child must learn that "no" can be powerful when he uses it the right way. Later he will use this word when he says "no" to peer pressure and drugs and to stay away from danger.

Your two-year-old will not know that following rules is how he learns. All he will know is that he wants his way. When you tell him "no," he will show his anger by crying and yelling. We will talk about this problem in Chapter 3.

Here are some things to remember:

- "No!" can mean a lot of things when a two-year-old child says it. It can mean: "I don't feel good," or "I need a nap," or "Let me play more," or "I need some attention." Listen to and look at your child. See why he is saying "no."

- Your two-year-old still needs to explore, just like when he was one. So you need to make your home safe for him. But you also need to watch your child when you are outside. He should not walk away by himself. Be extra careful where there are lots of people, such as on city streets. Your child may run off when you are not looking. It only takes a second for an accident to happen.

- Your two -year-old does not understand sharing. Two children will often want the same toy. This may cause small fights. Try to distract your child with another toy. Also try to have a toy for each child.

- Your child may be ready for potty training at this age. He should first be able to stay dry for two to three hours and pull his pants up and down by himself. You may need to wait until your child is 2 1/2- to 3 years old. That's OK. If you are worried, talk with a doctor or other professional about how to potty train. Note: Do not force your child or punish him when you are potty training. Instead, teach and encourage him.

Age 3: The Pal

At this stage your child will learn to play with others. She will learn what it means to have a friend. She will also learn about sharing and taking turns. The things she learns now will help her when she grows older.

Your three-year-old knows some of the rules now. She is learning more about herself and doing more for herself. But she will get angry when she cannot do some things other children can do. She may see a friend riding a bigger tricycle. Or she may see someone using scissors. If she cannot do these things, she may get angry. That is normal.

Your three-year-old has a great imagination. She may like to dress up in adult clothes. She will enjoy making up stories. She may also tell stories about herself that are not true. This is not lying. She is trying to learn the difference between the truth and "make-believe." She does not know that difference yet. Here are some things to remember:

- Your child needs to play with other children. That will help her learn to share and get along with others.

- Your three-year-old needs to have rules. For example, what happens if she refuses to take a nap? She still needs a nap, but she may not want one. She may fight with you. If she is too tired, she will not be fun to be around. She may fall asleep late in the afternoon and then not sleep through the night. Make sure you still set rules so this does not happen.

- Watch to see when she is getting hungry, tired, or bored. These feelings can affect her mood. So think ahead. Feed her, have her take a nap, or give her something to do before she gets cranky. When you think ahead, you will stop problems before they happen.

- Read books with her. She can look at the pictures and make up a story. This helps her learn. It is also a good time for you to be close to your child.

- Your three-year-old will get angry because she cannot do some things. Help her find the things she can do.

Age 4: The Adventurer

Your four-year-old is now ready to take risks. He is ready to learn what are safe risks and not-so-safe risks. He is also learning to take care of himself. He wants to see how fast he can go and how loud he can yell. He wants to see what he can do by himself.

Your four-year-old wants to know about everything. His mind is growing fast. He will ask "Why?" "Why?" "Why?" many times a day. Your answers will teach him about the world. He is also ready for pre-school. This is a great place for him to learn more about the world.

Your child moves faster now. He moves faster than he thinks. If you do not keep your eye on him, he may ride his bicycle into the street or run in front of a car. He still needs to hold your hand sometimes. You need to be sure he is safe. You should have rules he must obey. Here are some things to remember:

- Let him help do things for you and for himself. Encourage him for all the things he does, even if he makes a mistake. For example, say, "You tried really hard" or "Now that you tried pouring your own milk, why don't you try putting the cap back on the milk jug?"

- When you set rules for him, tell him what he may do before you tell him what he may not do. For example, say, "You may ride in the driveway, but not in the street" instead of "Don't ride in the street!" He needs to know what is OK for him to do.

- Your four-year-old still needs love and attention. You can hug him when you play together, when you watch TV, or when you put him to bed. Let him sit in your lap when you read him a book.

- Keep him busy with interesting things to do. He may want to color a picture or play a game. Offer him a choice of games, toys, and activities.

- Give him choices. For example, ask, "Do you want milk or water to drink?" or "Do you want to wear your blue sweater or your red jacket?" This will help him learn to make good choices.

Ages & Stages Chart

*Remember that all children are different. Some grow faster than others, and some grow slower than others. If your child is slower or faster than the chart, do not get upset. Be patient. If you have any concerns, ask your child's doctor or nurse.

Age Birth to 1: The Baby

Child's job #1:
To take in whatever she can— love, nourishment, attention, energy —to survive and thrive

Child's slogan:
"Love me by caring for my every need."

Parent's job #1:
To protect and nurture her because her life depends on it

- Helpless to survive and thrive on her own
- Needs your care…by design!
- Responds well to hugs, kisses, smiles, sweet talk, singing, reading, and other forms of nurture.
- Very active learner, always watching, listening, smiling, talking (or cooing), reaching
- Cries because she is hurting or needs something.
- Needs you to pay attention and respond when she wants to coo, babble, talk, or smile at you.
- Loves gentle movement like walking, rocking, and dancing.
- Loves gentle games and rhymes

Age 1: The Explorer

Child's job #1:
To get to know the world by seeing, hearing, touching, tasting, and smelling everything

Child's slogan:
"Check it out!"

Parent's job #1:
To provide safe places where he can explore

- Walks without help… then darts and dashes
- Reaches and tries to touch everything
- Puts everything in his mouth
- May bite, hit, or kick
- Doesn't understand "breakable"
- May be prone to injuries
- Says first words
- Sits in a chair by himself
- Knows different parts of the body
- Likes to pull things out of drawers
- Helps to put things away
- Is not ready to play well with other children

Age 2: The Boss

Child's job #1:
To test the limits of his new power

Child's slogan:
"I want what I want when I want it!"

- Wants to do more, try new things "by myself"
- May get angry or have tantrums
- Gets frustrated when she can't do things
- Likes to use the word "no"
- Tests everything: rules, your limits, her own skills
- Likes to run
- Opens doors using the doorknob

Age 2: The Boss, continued

Parent's job #1: Set limits firmly and calmly and allow the child freedom within those limits.	• Touches her body • Does not like to go to bed • Does not like to share • May be ready for potty training (but expect accidents!) • Likes to look at books and listen to you read • Likes to undress and run around without clothes

Age 3: The Pal

Child's job #1: To learn how to get along with others **Child's slogan:** "You've got a friend." **Parent's job #1:** To develop routines and provide opportunities for playing with others	• More able to follow rules and cooperate • Likes to play with others • Better at talking; may talk a lot • At times brave, at times insecure • May tell tall tales • Interrupts for attention • Can ride a tricycle or big wheel • Can sing a song • Asks a lot of questions • Sometimes shares toys and takes turns • Can unzip large zippers • Can talk about what she did yesterday • Will get angry if she cannot do things others do • May use the toilet but still wear a diaper at night

Age 4: The Adventurer

Child's job #1: To challenge himself and others **Child's Slogan:** "To boldly go where I have never gone before" **Parent's job #1:** To build on child's strengths while continuing to limit out-of-bounds behavior	• Always on the go, often "out of bounds" • Tests new skills and abilities • Plays make-believe, makes up stories • May get confused between what's true and not true • Sibling rivalry may be a problem • May challenge your authority • Asks "Why?" and many other questions • Can begin to copy big letters • Likes words, sounds, and rhymes • Can tell you where he lives • Can use a knife to cut some foods • Draws pictures of things he knows • May have bad dreams at night • Girls want to learn about boys; boys want to learn about girls

Your Child's Nature (Temperament)

Just because all children go through these ages and stages in the same order doesn't mean that all children are the same. Some children are born more outgoing than others, some more shy. Some are more aggressive while some are more laid back. And some are downright "spirited." The set of traits a child is born with is what we call the child's "nature" or "temperament," and it certainly affects a child's behavior. What happens to a child after he is born— in other words, his "experience," including how he is parented—also affects his behavior. Nature, experience, and the child's own free will all play a part in determining who your child becomes.

How much of who a child becomes is a product of nature and how much is a product of experience? That is still unknown. Most experts agree that young children try out many different behaviors as they seek to learn who they are. They are looking for a way to behave that best fits their own natures and also the environment in which they live. For example, a child with an aggressive temperament may try out hitting and bullying as a way of making a place for himself among other kids. He is not being bad. He is trying to be himself. However, in today's society he may find out that these behaviors get him into trouble, and he will not thrive that way. This is where parents and other caregivers can step in to provide guidance and set limits.

Some children are naturally easy-going and flexible. They seem to want to please and get along with other people. Such children are generally calm, happy and not easily upset. When something is bothering them, they may not show it or tell you. If you have an "easy" child, you may need to learn to listen with your eyes, as well as your ears, to know when they need help.

Some children are naturally more shy and like to keep to themselves. They need encouragement from parents and other caregivers to help them try new things or make friends. A positive attitude can help, too.

We cannot change a child's temperament, but we can help him adjust the way he behaves, and we can help him learn to get along with other people. A spirited child will probably grow into a spirited adult. The question is: Will he use his spirit to help himself and other people, or will he continue to get into trouble? The answer depends on what he learns from parents and other caregivers along the way. We will talk more about temperament and how to handle it in Chapter 3.

Parenting Styles

Just as there are many types of children, there are also many ways parents and other caregivers can teach them. We call these ways "parenting styles." Some styles are less helpful than others. They are either too hard or too soft on children. Like in the story of Goldilocks and the Three Bears, we need a parenting style that is "just right." Let's talk about the differences between these styles.

The "Too Hard" Style

Some parents want to control everything. They have too many rules. These parents use the "too hard" style. They do not let their children make many choices, and they punish them a lot. They do not give their children much in the way of hugs, kisses, or encouragement. Our grandparents may have used this style, but it does not work well today. When parents use the "too hard" style today, their children become angry. They do things just to make their parents angry, too. When they become teenagers they often rebel.

For example, Tricia is two years old. Her mother was watching a movie on TV. She told Tricia not to stand in front of the TV. But Tricia saw the bright lights and went over to have a look. Her mother yelled, "I told you to not to stand in front of the TV, Tricia!" Then she slapped Tricia"s behind. Tricia cried. Her mother said, "Stop crying! I can't hear my show!" Then Tricia cried more.

Her mother said, "If you don't stop crying, I will give you something to cry about!" So Tricia left the room with her head down. She cried softly to herself.

Tricia's mother used the "too hard" style. She thought Tricia should follow a rule when Tricia is too young to follow it. Then she got too angry when Tricia could not follow this rule.

The "Too Soft" Style

Parents who use the "too soft" style let their children run wild. They have too few rules. These parents may be too busy to teach their children, or they may not know how. They do not discipline their children. In fact, they may spoil their children when they let them do whatever they want, give them too many toys, or do things for them that their children could do for themselves. These children may get out of control.

WARNING: You cannot give your child too much love, such as hugs and encouragement. Love will never spoil your child. But you *can* give her too much freedom or too many toys.

For example, Raoul is four years old. One day when he was at the grocery store with his father, Raoul started running up and down the aisles of the store.

His father said softly, "Better not run, Raoul." But Raoul did not listen. He kept running… right into a stack of boxes, and they fell over. His father said, "Raoul, please stop," but Raoul kept running. His father picked up the boxes by himself.

Raoul said, "I want some ice cream."

"It's almost time for dinner," said his father.

"I don't care!" yelled Raoul. "I want some ice cream."

"OK," said his father. "If you will be quiet, I will get you some."

Raoul's father was being "too soft" when he let his son run wild in the store. He was "too soft" again when he let Raoul eat ice cream before dinner. Raoul's father did not set any rules.

The "Just Right" (or "Active") Style

Parents who use the "just right" style are not "too hard" or "too soft." They understand that their children need rules. They know that sometimes children make mistakes. This is part of learning. They give their children lots of love and encouragement. They let their children make some choices. Parents will make mistakes, too. When they make a mistake, they learn. The next time they will act differently.

For example, Mother hugs Tricia and says to her, "I am sorry I yelled and slapped you when you stood in front of the TV. You are more important to me than the movie. Let's find something you can do. Then you can sit next to me and play while I finish watching the movie." Of course, Mother will need to follow through by not getting angry or violent the next time Tricia misbehaves.

Raoul's dad can use the "just right" style too. He can say, "When we are in the store, we do not run. You can walk with me or ride in the shopping cart instead. You are a big boy now. You can help me put things in the cart. When we get the shopping done, maybe we can buy some fresh berries for dessert after dinner."

Most parents do not use just one style. Sometimes we are a little "too hard" and sometimes we are a little "too soft." Sometimes we are "just right." We will be better parents if we try to use the "just-right" style more and more. It is OK if we make mistakes. We learn from our mistakes. Our children learn when they make mistakes, too.

The Power of Choice

Part of a young child's job at any age is to become more and more independent. One "just right" way you can help teach your child to do this safely is to give her choices. Children want to decide some things for themselves. They do not want their parents to always tell them what to do. They also will say "no" a lot if you do not give them a chance to think and make choices.

You can give your child choices. This will help her grow and think. But she should not be free to make any choice. You decide what choices to give her. Give choices that are safe, healthy, and right for your child. For example, here is a parent giving no choice:

Parent:	"Here is your orange juice. Drink up."
Child:	"No, I hate it!"
Parent:	"I said drink it!"

The result: A power struggle.

Here is a parent giving a choice:

Parent:	"Would you like to have orange juice or apple juice this morning?"
Child:	"Apple juice."
Parent:	"Then apple juice it is."

The result: World peace. (Well, family peace anyway.)

When parents give choices, children:

- learn to use their power in good ways.

- are less likely to fight or rebel.

- learn how to make good decisions.

When you give choices, you teach your child to think.

Tips for Giving Choices

1. **Give only two choices at a time.** Young children are not ready for many choices. For example, ask, "Would you like corn flakes or oatmeal this morning?" Do not ask, "What do you want for breakfast?"

2. **The choices should be OK with you.** Do not give a choice of oatmeal or pancakes if you do not want to make pancakes. Also, give choices that are safe and healthy for your child's age.

3. **Do not make everything a choice.** Making decisions is hard work for children. If you give your child a lot of choices, it may be too much for her. Sometimes she just wants you to tell her what you want her to do.

✎ ✎ ✎ Choices Worksheet ✎ ✎ ✎

Write 3 commands you give your child, especially in problem areas such as bedtime or getting dressed in the morning. Then re-write these commands as choices. An example is included.

Command	Choice
Put on this shirt.	Would you like to wear this white shirt or the red one?
1.	
2.	
3.	

Give these choices to your child this week. After you try them, write down what happened. How did your child act?

1. _____

_____

_____

2. _____

_____

_____

3. _____

_____

_____

Building a Bond with Your Child

A bond with your child is a special connection. Even though you cannot see it, you can feel it with your heart when the bond is strong. It is a special feeling you have for your child. When you have a strong bond, you want to protect your child and teach him to be a responsible person. Your child wants to do things for you, too.

The bond starts when your child is born or even sooner (in the womb). As your child grows, the bond becomes stronger or weaker, depending on what kind of experiences you have with one another. When you are "too hard" or "too soft" as a parent, the bond becomes weaker. When you use the "just right" style, the bond becomes stronger. You build a strong bond when you give your child love and respect, when you care for her needs, hold her lovingly, work together, talk to her, and more. The bond also grows when you have fun with your child.

It is easier to teach your child when you have a strong bond. He will listen to you and obey your rules more often. He will like to be near you because he knows you love him. He will want to talk with you when he has a problem.

Love — Nurture — Connect

You are building the bond between you and your child when you...

- Play together.

- Laugh together.

- Hug, kiss, touch, cuddle.

- Talk to your baby/ talk with your child.

- Protect your child.

- Soothe, calm, and care for your child.

- Look lovingly into your child's eyes.

30

Bonding with Babies

When you build a bond with your baby, you form an attachment that will have lasting impact for both of you. Though it is never too late to build this bond, the sooner you start, the easier it will be. And one of the most important ways to start working on that bond early is by responding to your baby's needs.

How do you know when your baby needs something? Very simple: she cries. Crying means the baby needs you. What does she need? Well, that takes a little learning. Sometimes your baby will need to be fed; sometimes her diaper will need to be changed; sometimes she will be cold or hot; sometimes her tummy will hurt and she will need to be rocked, patted, or burped; sometimes she will be colicky and she will need you to follow your doctor's suggestions for helping her with it. Sometimes she may want you to talk with her or play games with her. As you learn what soothes your baby, you will also learn to tell what her different cries mean (though not all the time. Nobody is perfect at this!)

When your baby is crying but she is not in pain, hungry, in need of a diaper change, too hot or too cold, or colicky, what can you do to respond to her needs? Try some of these as you learn how to soothe her:

- Gentle touches

- Hugs and kisses

- "Talking" to her (cooing and crooning in response to the sounds she makes)

- Singing to her while rocking or dancing.

- Your own special "recipe"

As you bond with your child and learn what soothes her, your child is beginning to learn some important things about herself. She is experiencing emotions—or feelings. Let's take a closer look.

Paying Attention to Feelings

Feelings are a big part of what makes us human. We are not born knowing what feelings are, and yet as babies we begin to experience them. And as parents we see and hear the effect feelings have on our own babies, whether it's a cry that says, "I'm tired and grumpy" or a coo that says, "I'm happy," Feelings will play a big role in your child's life, starting from his very first cry.

Human beings have a wide range of feelings. Each of us feels things in our own unique way. But there are six emotions that are so much a part of the human experience that they show up in every culture on the planet. How do scientists know this? Because we all make the same faces when we experience them.

Can you guess the six universal emotions?
Use the photos as clues.

H_____

S_____

F_____

A_____

S_____

D_____

You may have had trouble getting the last feeling word, the one that starts with a D. Try imagining that you are about to take a bite out of an apple when you notice a big ugly worm coming out of it. What is the face you make and what is the feeling in the pit of your stomach? You

32

might even say, "Yuck, that's disgusting!" "Disgusted" is one of the six universal emotions. The others are: Happy, Sad, Fearful, Angry, and Surprised.

Why do we have feelings? Lots of reasons:

- Feelings give us information. They tell us what to avoid (like eating apples with worms) and what we want to do more of (like spending time with our children).

- Feelings motivate us to change things that are not working for us.

- Feelings give life color so that we can enjoy it more.

Getting to know our own feelings and our children's feelings is important. It is also important that we help our children learn to know what they are feeling and recognize other people's feelings, too. We will explore this more in Chapter 4, but for now, notice what your child is feeling. You can do this by paying attention to his facial expressions, tone of voice, words, and behavior (or misbehavior). These are the most common ways people show their feelings.

Every Day, a Little Play

Play with your child every day. Playing a few minutes a day is better than playing once a week for an hour. Even if playing is new for you, you can learn to play and enjoy your child's laughter. After all, it's one of the joys of being a parent! When you play with your child, you:

- Build her self-esteem.

- Help her learn about the world.

- Help her learn new skills.

- Help build the bond between you.

- Have fun together!

Keep in mind that playing with a baby is different than playing with a four-year-old. Each child at each stage will be different. On the next page there is a list of games you can play with your child at each age. You can also make up your own games. Your child may have a game she loves to play over and over again.

You might think you do not have time to play with your child every day. When you have a busy day, you can find time to play while you are doing other things such as driving, buying groceries, or giving your child a bath. Making things fun will help your child want to do these things, too!

What games do you and your child enjoy playing now?

_____

_____

_____

_____

_____

The Playing to Learn Chart on pages 36-37 will give you some more ideas for toys, games, and activities that fit your child's age and stage.

Brain-Building Activity: Follow the Lead

Playing is how children learn. They learn from every kind of play, but we can help them learn even more with what we call "smart play." In each chapter we will learn a new game or activity you can do with your children that triggers growth and development in their brains.

Following your child's lead is an important kind of smart play. It sounds like what it means: When you follow your child's lead, you do whatever your child wants to do.

Why is following the lead such an important thing to do with your child? It has been proven to help children's brains develop in many healthy ways. For example it improves their self-control, the way they handle their feelings, and how they feel about themselves.

Here are two games that involve following your child's lead.

Mirroring

You and your child stand facing each other. When your child moves, move with him as if you are his image in the mirror. Follow his lead and mirror every movement he makes, even the expression on his face!

AGE GUIDELINES: This activity is appropriate for children age one and older. Younger children may not understand this as a game, but they will still enjoy having movements mirrored and will benefit from the activity. Allow your child to set the pace and the type of movement and actions involved.

Make-Believe Tea Party

Sit across a table from your child and have a make-believe tea party. Your child takes the lead by serving pretend tea and food and asking you for items, and you follow her by taking what she offers, responding to her movements and what she says, and enjoying the party!

AGE GUIDELINES: This activity is appropriate for children age three and older. Allow your child to set the pace and the type of movement and actions involved.

Playing to Learn Chart

	Birth to 1	Age 1
Blocks	Large blocks of foam or other soft material in different colors Your child learns: • to notice color, texture, weight, and sound (of banging blocks together) • to pick up and drop • to knock down and throw soft objects	Your child will line them up, stack them, and knock them down Your child learns: • how to use her hands • what happens when she hits the blocks • how to build things • how to put things in order
Books	Picture books of animals and everyday things; books with rhymes and things she can touch Your child learns: • the sound of words and voices (the beginning of language skills) • the feeling of textures (in some books) • to cuddle up and be close with you	Picture books of animals, cars, places, and everyday things; books with rhymes Your child learns: • to listen as you read • the sounds of words • to say her first words
Music	Simple songs, nursery rhymes, songs with hand movements. Try different types of music (lullaby, soft, slow, peppy, etc.) to see what your baby likes! Your child learns: • to listen to music • to hear sounds, rhythms, and how words sound with music	Simple songs and nursery rhymes. Songs with finger and hand movements Your child learns: • to recognize sounds and rhythms • to imitate sounds and hand movements (clapping, patty cake, bye-bye)
Objects	Mobiles, stuffed animals, rattles, containers, measuring spoons on a ring, stacking rings, nesting cups, shape sorters Your child learns: • muscle control, coordination • color, texture, shape, size, and weight • how to make things happen	Plastic containers to stack, nest, fill up, and empty; lids, blocks, simple puzzles, and things with different shapes Your child learns: • how each part works • that some things fit into other things • that some things fit on top of other things
Pretend	Games and toys that involve hiding and reappearing (peek-a-boo, jack in the box) Your child learns: • to look for the object that has been hidden	Dolls, stuffed animals, old clothes, blankets, pretend adult items (toy phone, kitchen tools) Your child learns: • how to act • how other people and animals act
Touch and Feel Things	Balls and blocks with different surfaces; teething ring Your child learns: • that there is a world outside of herself • to touch and feel things • to use her hands and fingers • how objects are different from one another	Containers he can fill up and empty, soft cloth, sticky things, cold things, sand, rice Your child learns: • more about his world through feeling and touching • more about hard and soft, wet and dry, empty and full

Age 2	Age 3	Age 4
Large wooden blocks, big Legos™ with little people, animals, cars Your child learns: • to think and create • more control of her hands and body	Small square blocks to make towers, large blocks to make roads, buildings or tunnels Your child learns: • to balance things • to think about	All sizes of blocks and boxes, toys with different shapes that fit together Your child learns: • to plan and build • how to solve problems
Simple, short stories with a beginning, a middle, and an end Your child learns: • to talk and listen • to tell stories with new words	Books with pictures and 2 or 3 sentences on each page Your child learns: • to recognize letters, which will help her learn to read later	Silly and funny books, rhyming books, stories about children or animals, stories about simple problems Your child learns: • that words and letters have different sounds
Songs, playing with your fingers, drums you make. Your child learns: • to practice new words and sounds • to follow directions	Songs with motion. Your child learns: • to use words, sound, and body movements together	Children's songs; pots, pans, boxes, drums, and other things to make noise with Your child learns: • that songs have rhythm • that her voice has different tones
Play-dough, plastic cookie cutters, rolling pin, balls, large cardboard boxes Your child learns: • to think about what he is doing	8-10 piece puzzles, bright beads that snap together, things with different shapes Your child learns: • how things fit together • how colors look together • how to put things in order	Smaller beads to string together, children's scissors, puzzles Your child learns: • to make hands and eyes work together • to work slowly and carefully
Dolls, doll clothes, empty food boxes, mail you do not want Your child learns: • how adults act	Toy telephone, toy dishes, old clothes Your child learns: • about adults by acting like adults	Old clothes, dolls, doll clothes, puppets, masks, costumes Your child learns: • that some things are pretend and some things are real
Helping you cook simple things Your child learns: • about hot and cold, sticky, wet, soft • how to follow directions	Finger paints, clay, colored markers, and markers that have different smells Your child learns: • to use her hands, fingers, and her mind to make different things	Water and sand with pails and shovels, plastic tubes, art supplies Your child learns: • that she can make things happen • how things feel • how things move

Taking Care of Yourself

You have a big job taking care of your children. But who takes care of you? You do. That is part of your job as a parent. When you take good care of yourself, you will have energy and will feel happier. This will help you take care of your child.

Taking care of yourself is called "self-care." Self-care means that you get enough sleep, eat healthy food, and do things that make you happy. This helps keep you fresh and healthy. Your child needs you this way.

Each day you give a lot of energy to other people and your children. You need to give yourself some energy, too. But can you give yourself too much care? Yes.

Some parents spend too much time taking care of themselves. They do not give enough to their children. Other parents give too much to their children. They do not have enough energy for themselves. When you are a "just right" parent, you give time to your children **and** to yourself.

Here are some ways you can give yourself self-care:

- Healthy body
- Healthy mind
- Talk and visit with other people.
- Get organized.

If you have a child with special needs, you need to be especially careful about taking care of yourself. It may be easy for you to get so concerned about your child that you forget that you can't be a good parent if you don't take care of yourself, too. Make sure that you know what help is available in your community and take advantage of it. Don't try to do everything yourself. It's not only OK to get the help you need; it's in the best interest of your child.

✎✎✎ Self-Care Chart ✎✎✎

Healthy body

1. Eat healthy food.
2. Do not drink a lot of alcohol.
3. Get enough sleep.
4. Exercise.
5._____
6._____
7._____
8._____
9._____
10._____

Talk and visit with other people.

1. Talk with other parents once a week.
2. Spend time with your friends.
3. Find someone to talk to about problems.
4. Have fun. _____
5._____
6._____
7._____
8._____
9._____
10._____

Healthy mind

1. When things get too wild, stop. Try to relax and be calm.
2. Spend time outdoors. Take a walk; go to the park; sit by a lake.
3. Relax! Take a bath, listen to music, or read.
4._____
5._____
6._____
7._____
8._____
9._____
10._____

Get organized.

1. Make a to-do list each day.
2. Keep a calendar to mark times and places where you have to be.
3. Take time to organize each part of your home.
4._____
5._____
6._____
7._____
8._____
9._____
10._____

Now choose one new self-care activity to do for yourself this week. Write this activity here. Enjoy it! This is for you.

_____

_____

_____

Introduction to Mindfulness

One reason that self-care is so important for parents is that parenting can be stressful. Too much stress is not only harmful to you; it can also be harmful to your children. So it's important that you have ways to reduce stress in your life. That is where mindfulness can help.

Mindfulness is...
paying attention
fully
in the present moment
on purpose.

Mindfulness can help you:

- Calm your strong feelings by moving through them.

- Manage stress.

- Stay present—in relationships and in life.

- Be at your best with your children.

Mindfulness can help your children:

- Soothe themselves when they are upset.

- Pay attention for longer.

- Focus on what is important.

Mindfulness is a powerful tool. It can be helpful in all kinds of situations, but it is especially good at reducing stress. Practicing mindfulness regularly can improve your relationships and strengthen your bond with your children. And teaching your children how to be mindful can help them be calmer, happier, and more focused. Each chapter of this guide will include a Mindful Moment: an exercise that will help both you and your child practice mindfulness.

Mindful Moment: The Mind Jar

Our first Mindful Moment is about finding your breath. This is an activity you can do by yourself or with a child (see age guidelines at the end of the activity). Making a "mind jar" and using it during the breathing exercise will help you and your child learn what mindfulness is and how it can help you.

1. Make a mind jar.

You will need:

> A clear plastic jar with a tight-fitting lid
> Warm water
> Clear craft glue (for example, Elmer's Clear School Glue)
> Colorful glitter

Child safety note:

Glitter can be a choking hazard. Do not leave children unsupervised with a mind jar. Store it in a locked cabinet or somewhere children cannot access, even with a step stool.

Directions:

Fill the jar with warm water. Add clear glue and stir. The glue will dissolve quickly and make the water thicker. Add the glitter to the jar and close it tightly.

Imagine that this jar represents your mind. When something stressful happens…

Shake up your mind jar and set it down. How does it look?

See the glitter swirling around? That is what your thoughts and feelings are doing inside your mind: swirling around, distracting you, and making you feel stressed.

2. Find your breath.

The purpose of this exercise is to find your breath. Through your breathing, you will calm those swirling thoughts.

Find a comfortable position sitting on the floor or in a chair with your hands relaxing in your lap, eyes slightly open, not quite focused but looking at something a few feet in front of you.

Breathe in through your nose to the count of four. Notice your breath as it comes in through your nose. Allow it to fill your lungs deeply. Try to breathe in so your belly expands.

1 … 2 … 3 … 4 …

Hold the breath for a few seconds, then allow the breath to release for a count of seven.

1… 2… 3… 4… 5… 6… 7…

Take three or four of these deep breaths.

Notice what has happened in your mind jar while you were breathing. The glitter has settled to the bottom, just as your swirling thoughts and feelings have settled in your mind.

Finding your breath is a powerful tool for bringing yourself into the present moment. We *all* get distracted. No one can stay present all the time. The practice will help you notice when you are not present in this moment and gently guide you back to it.

When you become mindful of your body and your breathing, your stressful thoughts settle down and your mind calms. Those thoughts and feelings can still be there in your mind, but they are not in charge anymore. You are in charge.

Mindfulness is a skill that will take very little time to practice, but it's important that you practice it often. If you do it daily, it will get easier and feel more natural. Your mind will get better at noticing when you are focused in the present and when you are not.

AGE GUIDELINES: This activity is appropriate for children ages two and older. Though young children may not be able to understand the idea of mindfulness, they will still benefit from the breathing exercise.

Home Activities

Check the box beside each activity after you complete it this week:

- ☐ I will take care of myself.
- ☐ I will play with my child.
- ☐ I will give my child choices.
- ☐ I will follow my child's lead.
- ☐ I will practice my mindfulness exercises.
- ☐ I will read Chapter 1 and complete the activities.

Do these 6 things at home this week, then answer these questions:

After I gave myself some self-care, I felt: _____

_____

_____

After I played with my child, I felt: _____

_____

_____

This is what happened when I gave my child choices: _____

_____

_____

This is what happened when I practiced following my child's lead:

_____

_____

_____

After I practiced my mindfulness exercises, I felt: _____

_____

_____

2 Preventing Problems

Problems are a part of life.

This chapter is about problems. Nobody really likes problems, but every family has them. Some problems can be prevented. Other problems can be solved. One good thing about problems is that they can help us teach our children about life. So this chapter is really about using problems as teaching situations to help your child learn how to survive and thrive.

Humans may not be the only creatures on Earth that can solve problems (Ever seen a squirrel raiding a "squirrel-proof" bird feeder?), but we are capable of solving far more complex problems than any other animal, That is because the human brain is far more complex than any other animal's.

Your Child's Beautiful Brain

Your child's brain is amazing! It has billions of tiny cells made for learning how to survive and thrive. Many of these cells (called *neurons*) are already connected when a baby is born. These connections are what let her know how to do basic things like breathe, suck, swallow, and poop. She will make lots of other connections on her own as she experiences more of life.

Nature prepares a child's brain for learning by giving it far more connections than it will ever use. As the child learns and experiences things, the connections she uses get stronger. The connections she does not use fall away.

Early childhood is the most critical period for this building-up and trimming-down process in the brain. It's when a child is most capable of learning. So to help your child build a good, strong brain, it's important that you provide learning opportunities and positive experiences during her first few years. Even better is when learning opportunities and positive experiences happen together so that the brain connects learning with pleasure. Positive experiences with parents and other caregivers actually help to build babies' brains!

Let's look at how a child's brain develops. It helps to think of it as having three parts, and they develop from the bottom up:

The Old Brain: When a baby is born, the most developed area of its brain is at its base, where the brain meets the spine. This is called the "old" brain because it has been part of humans and other mammals for millions of years. It controls those basic functions of the body we mentioned earlier. It also makes us ready to fight or run when we see danger.

The Emotional Brain: This part of the brain develops next, triggering the experience of new emotions. In the second six months of life, the baby begins to feel and show fear and anger. Later come joy, caring, love, and bonding, to name a few.

The Rational Brain: Emotions help us in a lot of ways, but they need to be controlled. The rational brain does that and much more. Think of it like the Manager of the brain. It is in charge of things like:

- Making good decisions
- Feeling for others (empathy)
- Learning from consequences
- Controlling emotions
- Morality (knowing right from wrong)

The rational brain will not finish developing until around age 25. It is the last part of the brain to develop. This is important because the rational brain is where our best thinking goes on. So if you ever get frustrated because your child is not good at making decisions, knowing right from wrong, or any of the higher-level thinking skills, remember that it takes a long time for the brain to fully develop. And brain development goes along with muscle development and physical growth. So don't expect your child to be able to do or understand what adults, or even older children, can do! That will just make them stressed and angry.

46

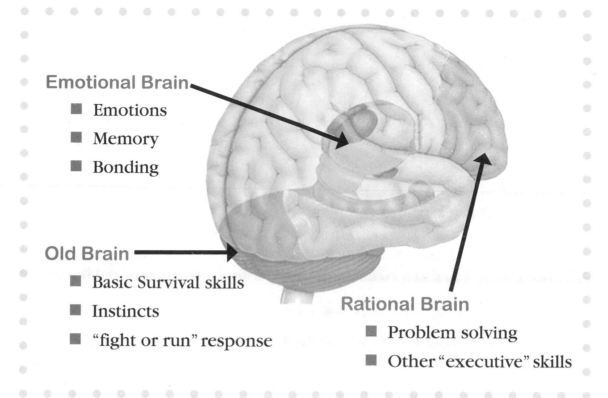

Emotional Brain
- ■ Emotions
- ■ Memory
- ■ Bonding

Old Brain
- ■ Basic Survival skills
- ■ Instincts
- ■ "fight or run" response

Rational Brain
- ■ Problem solving
- ■ Other "executive" skills

When a child gets stressed out, the brain releases chemicals to help the body deal with it. For kids who experience abuse, neglect, or violence, their brains are constantly producing these chemicals. The chemicals may be helpful in small doses, but too much can actually slow down brain development. This is what we call *toxic stress*. It can have a lasting negative impact on a child, especially if it happens during the first few years.

On the other hand, when parents hug or play with a young child, the brain releases other chemicals that help the child bond with you and makes them feel safe and secure. This has the opposite effect of toxic stress. It improves brain development and strengthens the bond between parent and child.

This doesn't mean that all stress is bad. In fact, some stress is good. But without the nurturing and guidance of loving parents and other caregivers, children would be lucky to survive, and they certainly wouldn't thrive.

Brain-Building Activity: Freeze Dance

Have you ever been about to do or say something but then you stopped yourself? You thought for a moment and decided that it would be better if you didn't do or say it. This ability to pause and think is at the foundation of good decision making. Children are not born with this ability. They have to learn it. You can help them learn it. And as you know, children learn through play.

Playing Freeze Dance with your child is a way to exercise the part of his brain that learns to pause and think before taking action. Like a muscle, when we exercise it, it gets stronger.

To play Freeze Dance, you will need an open space (for example, a living room with the furniture moved aside), a music player, and some lively music to play. You can play it with one child, but it works best with several children.

The rules are simple:

 When the music is playing, dance!

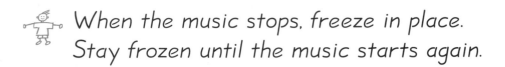 When the music stops, freeze in place. Stay frozen until the music starts again.

AGE GUIDELINES: This activity is appropriate for children age two and older. Adjust the difficulty depending on age and ability. For beginners or very young children, start by playing the music for long periods with only occasional freezes until the children get good at stopping and freezing. As they learn the game, play shorter and shorter music segments. If they do well, start making it harder by varying the length of time they dance and freeze.

Mindful Moment: Relaxation and Breathing Exercises

When you stop and calm your thoughts and feelings, you give yourself the chance to think about the things you say and do. This helps you make better decisions. In the Mindful Moment for Chapter 1, you learned how to find your breath. Now you will learn three techniques for using your breath to bring yourself to the present and calm both your mind and your body.

Your child will benefit from these breathing exercises, too. They are easy to teach, and they will calm your child's thoughts and feelings when he is upset or over-stimulated. Plus, practicing mindfulness is another way for your child to learn the important skill of pausing to think before acting

Children will learn these breathing techniques best when they are calm. Do not try to teach your child when he is upset. Once he has had time to practice and get familiar with the techniques, he will be more able to use them to calm himself when upset.

Also make sure *you* are calm before you teach your child any of the following skills (or any skill, for that matter). Take a few minutes to do a mindfulness exercise yourself. Calm yourself and bring yourself to the present.

Breathing Exercise #1. Butterfly Breath

Think about how a butterfly looks when it sits on a branch, slowly opening and closing its wings. Keep that image in your mind.

Stand up and lightly press the palms of your hands together in front of your chest, as if praying. This is your "wings closed" position. Inhale deeply as you slowly "open your wings." Move your hands apart until your palms are facing forward and your thumbs are in line with your shoulders. Your back is tense. Hold this position for a few seconds.

Then slowly exhale and bring your hands back together. Allow your back muscles to relax as you move your hands back to their original position, gently touching in front of your chest.

Repeat three times.

Breathing Exercise #2. Windy Woods

For this exercise, you will stand and make believe that you are a tree in the woods.

Take a deep breath, filling your lungs completely all the way down to your belly. As you inhale, lift your arms up over your head.

Now sway like a tree in the wind. Slowly exhale through your mouth, making the sound of the wind. Lower your arms as you finish exhaling.

Repeat three times.

Breathing Exercise #3. Balloon Breath

For this exercise, you will stand and make believe you are a balloon letting its air out.

Put your hands on your shoulders. As you inhale deeply, letting your belly expand, extend your arms up over your head with your elbows slightly bent. Hold that position for a few seconds.

As you exhale slowly through your mouth, make the sound of the balloon losing air—"p-p-p-p-p-p-p" (like blowing a raspberry). Slowly empty your lungs and lower your arms until you have exhaled all the air and your hands are back in their original position on your shoulders.

Repeat three times.

AGE GUIDELINES: These three breathing exercises are appropriate for children age two and older. For younger children, do the breathing exercises facing the child, making eye contact with him and encouraging him to imitate whichever parts he can.

Keeping Your Child Safe and Sound

When we described the "just right" parenting style we said that Job #1 is protecting your child. This means you need to prevent problems before they happen as often as you can. Young children want to learn and know everything. They do not understand that the world can be dangerous. It is up to you to teach your child what is safe and what is not. This starts with your home.

Your home can be dangerous to a young child. For example, your child may want to know what is in the hole in the toilet. She may want to play with the water. She does not know she could get her hand stuck or even fall in. You need to keep her from playing in the toilet.

Keeping your child safe is a big job. Keeping your house safe is a good way to start. Put anything that could break and hurt your child out of their sight and reach. This is called "child proofing." It means you make your house safe before your child gets hurt. You will not have to say "no" to your child as often.

Never leave a young child at home alone. If there is a fire or medical problem, your child must have a responsible adult or caregiver there to help. Be sure that you know your child's caregiver well. Do not leave your child with anyone you think might get mad and hurt her. And if you take your child to a childcare center, check to make sure it is a healthy and safe place. Read more about finding good childcare on page 58.

Being safe away from home is important, too. When you are in a car, everyone must wear a seat belt. It's the law in the United States. Never have more people in a car than you have seat belts. Young children must also be in a safety seat (typically up to age four) or a booster seat (typically up to age five).

You may think that you can hold your child safely in your lap. Research on car crashes shows that you can't. There is too much force and she will fly out of your hands before you know what happened.

Also, never leave a young child in a car alone. Do not leave her even for a few minutes. Bad things happen fast. A car can get very hot very fast. Children's bodies cannot cope with hot or cold temperatures like adults' bodies. The inside of a shut-up car can get hot enough to kill an infant or child within minutes. This can happen even during cold weather. Even in cold weather, leaving a child alone in a car can be deadly.

Important things to remember about safety seats and belts for babies and young children[1]:

- Always use a child safety seat and a seat belt. You may be able to get a free or reduced-cost car seat for your child from a public healthcare organization. Call your county or state health department and request information about this.

- Know your state's laws about seat belts, safety seats, and booster seats. Two good online resources for parents on car seat safety are the National Highway Traffic Safety Administration's website and the American Academy of Pediatrics page on car seat safety. Look them up!

- Strap the car seat to the car with the seat belt. Make sure it fits tightly. Strap your child to the car seat.

- Read and follow all instructions that come with your car seat. All people caring for your child should know how to use the seat correctly.

- Around age four your child may be ready for a booster seat. This makes him tall enough to use the regular seat belts. Booster seats help prevent injuries by keeping your child snug in his seat if there is an accident.

1   Laws for child safety seats and booster seats differ by state in the U.S., depending on the age, weight, and height of the child. Children that are small for their age might need to be in a safety seat or a booster even if they are past the age requirement.

Infant Safety

☐ Before you bring your baby home, discuss her car seat with the hospital staff. They can make recommendations for the right size and shape of car seat you need for your child.

☐ In the first two months of life, babies can't hold their heads up well. Be sure your baby has proper head support at all times. When you are holding her in your arms or in a sling, her face should be visible and close enough to kiss. When she is in a rear-facing car seat, it is best that someone rides in the back seat with her to make sure that her head does not slump over. This could block her air passage.

☐ Premature babies are especially at risk, so be sure to ask for special instructions at the hospital or from your baby's pediatrician.

☐ Follow all **sleep safety rules** for babies, including:

■ Place your baby on his back to sleep.

■ Use a safety-approved crib with a safety-approved mattress.

■ Do not put pillows, blankets, a bumper, stuffed animals, or other items in the crib with your baby.

■ Change your baby into a sleep suit to keep him warm and comfortable.

■ Newborns and young infants should share the room with parents but should not share a bed with parents or anyone else. Place the baby's crib next to the parents' bed.

☐ Please remember that this list and all our safety suggestions are not exhaustive. Talk to your baby's pediatrician to get the best advice for keeping her safe.

Safe Home Checklist

Read this list. Then go through your home, doing what has not been done. Put a check in each box as you do it. As your child grows, you will need to re-check this list to make sure that you have adjusted your home to match your child's increasing size and ability to reach things.

Living Room

☐ Cover electrical outlets with plastic outlet covers (you can buy these in most stores).

☐ Take away small rugs so your child will not trip, or put rubber pads under them so the rugs do not slip.

☐ Put padding on the sharp edges of the table (use foam pads). If you cannot pad the table or do not want to, remove the table until your child is older.

☐ Some plants are poisonous. Put them on a high shelf that your child cannot reach.

☐ Cords on drapes should be short. Your child should not be able to reach them. If there are loops on cords, cut them.

☐ Put away anything that can break.

☐ Check all shelves and things your child can climb on. The shelves should be strong and not fall over.

☐ Put a screen in front of the fireplace and teach your child that this is not a place to play in. Put padding over the sharp edges of the hearth.

Kitchen

☐ Take knobs off the stove when you are not using it.

☐ Put sharp knives and kitchen scissors in a place your child cannot reach or open.

☐ Put matches in a place your child cannot reach or open.

☐ When you are cooking, try to use only the back burners. Turn pan handles inward so your child cannot reach them and pull the pots off the stove.

☐ Put all cleaners, paints, and detergents in a cabinet with a child safety lock (you can buy a child safety lock in many stores).

☐ Do not use cleaners near your child (the smell can make him sick or burn his skin).

☐ If your child swallows poison, call Poison Control immediately.

☐ Unplug everything when you are not using it (toaster, iron, blender, and so on).

☐ Keep all plastic bags and garbage bags in a place your child cannot reach or open.

☐ Wipe up all spilled liquid from the floor as soon as it happens.

Bathroom

☐ Keep caps on all bottles. Always use child-proof safety caps. Ask your pharmacist to use them for all prescription medications.

☐ Lock up all medicines (vitamins, aspirin, alcohol, laxatives and so on). All vitamins—even children's—are very important to lock up because the iron in them is poisonous to young children.

☐ Put rubber mats in the bath tub or shower to prevent slipping.

☐ Keep a bath mat next to the bath tub and shower.

☐ Put a toilet lid latch on the toilet if your child likes to reach in.

☐ If you can, lower the temperature of your hot water heater to 120° F at the most. The hot water should not be able to burn your hand. If you cannot change the water temperature, use a hot water faucet guard (you can buy these in many stores). Be sure your faucets cannot be turned on easily.

** Important: Never leave a child alone in the bath tub.

Child's Bedroom

☐ Look at all toys. Take away all toys with broken or sharp edges. Also take away toys with pieces smaller than a big walnut.

☐ Use only toys that are right for your child's age.

☐ Make sure windows cannot open.

☐ Cover electrical outlets.

Stairs

☐ If you have a young child, put a gate at the top and bottom of the stairs.

☐ Keep stairs clear of toys, papers, and other objects.

Garage or Workroom

☐ Put away all tools so your child cannot reach them.

☐ Put paints, cleaners, and other chemicals in a place your child cannot reach or open.

☐ Lock up all poisons.

☐ Put nails and screws in a place your child cannot reach or open.

Laundry Room

☐ Always close washing machine and dryer doors.

☐ Keep detergents and fabric softeners out of reach.

Other Things to Check

☐ Garbage cans should be kept in a locked closet or high off the floor.

☐ Have smoke alarms and carbon monoxide alarms in the house. Check them every month. Change the batteries twice a year when the time changes.

☐ Have fire extinguishers in the house and know how to use them.

☐ Practice how to get out of the house if there is a fire. Remember to crawl on the floor (where there is less smoke). Have an escape plan.

☐ Put these numbers by your telephone: poison control, fire, police, emergency medical services, pediatrician.

☐ Do not leave children unsupervised around bath tubs, hot tubs, pools (including baby pools), ponds and lakes, streams and rivers, and other water. Babies, young, children, and weak swimmers should always have an adult swimmer within arm's reach. Even if they know how to swim, young children should not be left alone around water.

Playing Safe Checklist

Part of preventing problems is to make sure that the toys and other objects your child has to play with are safe. Here are some safe things your child can do in different parts of the home:

Kitchen

☐ Let your child play in a low drawer. That will be her drawer. Put safe things, such as pots, pans, and cartons, in that drawer for her. She will have something safe to do when you are working in the kitchen.

Bathroom

☐ Always supervise children around a bathtub when there is water in it.

☐ Put a low, safe stool in the bathroom for your child. Let him use it when he is learning to wash his hands. He can also use it when he brushes his teeth.

Bedroom or Living Room

☐ Make some low shelves for your child. You can use colorful plastic crates to hold the shelves. Use these shelves to store your child's toys. She will be able to see the toys here and will want to play with them more.

☐ Use a shoebox to store your child's small toys. Draw or cut out a picture of the toys. Then glue it on the shoebox. Your child will learn that all the farm animals will go in the box with the picture of the farm animals on it. The blocks will go in the box with the picture of the blocks on it.

☐ When your child no longer puts things in her mouth, have a basket of magazines and colorful paper your child can use. Let her tear them, cut them, or color them. These magazines are just for her.

☐ Put up a low hook with a blunt, plastic end. Your child can hang up his coat or sweater there.

☐ Put a basket in your child's room. Teach him to put his dirty clothes in the basket.

Other Ideas for Playing Safe:

_____

_____

_____

_____

Finding Good Childcare

Whether you are working full time, part time, or just need a good baby sitter from time to time, who you trust your child with when they are not with you is very important. Why? Because:

Your child's health and safety always come first. We talked about the importance of child proofing your own home and making sure your children are safe and healthy. So it is also important that anyone who watches your children should be someone you trust, someone who knows and cares about child safety.

Your child's emotional wellbeing is important, too. The caregiver you choose will spend a lot of time with your child. This person will have a strong effect on how your child thinks and feels and how she develops. You want caregivers who will nurture your child with love and respect, who will play with your child and teach her things. You do not want caregivers who sit your child in front of a TV all day or worse, yell and scream at your child.

No child learns everything he needs from his parents. There are risks in having others care for your child, but there are also opportunities. Children can learn many life lessons from other caring adults. They can learn everything from how to follow rules, to getting along with others, to academic skills. So as much as possible, put your child around others who can help build a sense of belonging, learning and contributing.

Tips on finding good childcare:

1. Talk to other parents. The easiest way to get started in a search for good childcare is to ask other parents. It is best to ask parents you know and trust, but even internet reviews can give you some ideas about where to look.

2. Make a visit and then look, ask, think. Arrange to visit the childcare center or interview the person who will be staying with your child in your home. Watch how the teachers interact with the children and how they handle problems. Ask good questions. As you

58

tour the center and interview caregivers, ask yourself: is this a place you can really trust to nurture and teach your child? Pay attention to your feelings with this and trust any warning signs you sense.

3. Look for a child-friendly, stimulating environment. Every place has its "atmosphere" or feel. You want one that is child-friendly with plenty of toys, games, learning opportunities, and other positive stimulation to help grow your child's beautiful brain. But even more than that, ask yourself if this is a place (or person) that seems to "get" children. In fact…

4. Look for people who seem to really like children. Your child will thrive around people who like children, especially when they like your child in particular. Unfortunately, not every teacher or childcare professional really likes children. If you can watch how they act with children, you have a good chance to tell if they seem to really enjoy their work. If you can only interview them, ask questions such as, "Why did you decide to go into childcare?", "What do you like about your job?", and "What *don't* you like about it?"

5. Work cooperatively with the teachers and/or provider. Once you have chosen a childcare provider, your job is not over. It's important to continue to talk with them, observe them in action, and problem-solve together. Become a good team. Always be respectful, but if you find that in spite of your best efforts it is not working as you think it should, be open to change. There are other centers and other caregivers who might be a better fit.

Teaching your child is important.

We said earlier that your child's brain comes with billions of cells waiting to be connected. Making these connections is what we mean by "learning." How do you teach your child to share, take turns, and obey the rules? Children need to learn these things so they can work and cooperate with others. This will help them prevent problems and grow up healthy and happy. If they do not learn these things, they will have many more problems and may be unhappy. If you teach your child how to behave, you will love to be around her, and so will other people!

We will suggest some ways to teach your child how to act responsibly. These methods have worked for millions of parents. They will work for you, too, but it will take time and practice. Do not stop if these methods do not work the first time. Keep trying them, and your child will change. You may be doing some things now that work with your child. Good for you! Or you may decide not to use some of our methods. That's OK. You are the parent, and you should decide.

Getting Discipline "Just Right"

All children misbehave sometimes. They are learning about the world, about you, and about themselves. Sometimes they break your rules. Your job is to teach your child to learn without breaking the rules. Sometimes, young children think about themselves only. We want to teach them to think about other people sometimes and what they need. We also want to teach young children how to do more things for themselves.

Teaching is sometimes called discipline. In fact, discipline means teaching. It does not mean hurting your child when he makes you mad.

Do not hurt your child by:

- yelling at him.

- calling him names.

- using bad language.

- threatening him.

- shaking him.*

- hitting or spanking him.

IMPORTANT: Shaking or hitting your child can cause serious injury or even death. Shaking can rattle a child's brain so that it hits the inside of his skull. This can cause brain damage, a coma, or even death. NEVER SHAKE A BABY OR CHILD.

These methods are sometimes used by parents with a **"Too Hard" style** of parenting. (Sometimes it gets so "hard" that it is actually child abuse.) All of these examples hurt children. It can harm their bodies, and it hurts their feelings. It also hurts the bond you are building with your child. It can even teach your child to misbehave more! Your parents may have treated you this way. But you do not have to treat your child this way.

Again, discipline means teaching. But you are not teaching your child the right thing when you use a **"Too Soft" style** of parenting either. Such parents often ignore misbehavior. Or maybe they are not clear about rules, or they give in to the child too often, or they do not use any discipline at all.

What happens to kids who grow up with a "too soft" approach?

- They have trouble learning right from wrong.

- They have trouble accepting rules.

- They become spoiled.

- They get into trouble.

You can choose to teach your child in better ways than these. You can choose to show love and respect for your child, even when you discipline him. You can use the **"Just Right"** (or Active) style of parenting. This style begins with preventing misbehavior and then using respectful, non-violent discipline when it is needed.

Some tips on how to prevent your child from misbehaving:

- Help him stay busy, not bored. (Take crayons or a toy with you when you will be someplace where he will have to wait.)

- Tell him what you want him to do, not just "don't do that."

- Show him how to act; don't just tell him.

- Anticipate when he will be hungry, tired, or fussy when planning errands.

- Stick to a routine when possible.

- Care for the child's needs and your own.

Listening to What Your Child Needs

Sometimes children misbehave because they are too tired, hungry, hot, cold, bored, wet, in pain, or have some other need they cannot take care of by themselves. The younger they are, the less able they are to tell you what the problem is. That's the main reason a baby cries. It tells you she needs something.

For example, in Chapter 1 we talked about how babies cry when they need something. They might be hungry and saying, "Feed me!" Or they might be saying, "I'm hot or cold. Put something on or off me." "I'm wet. Change me." "I'm tired. Put me to bed." "I'm just feeling irritable. Calm me."

When your baby cries, don't ignore it. Find out what she needs and meet that need for her. This will help her grow into a confident, secure child.

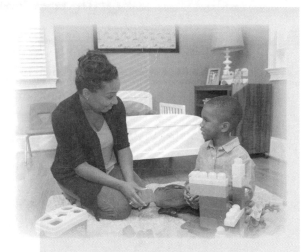

Even older children sometimes do not really know why they are upset. They may act fussy and whiny because they are tired or hungry. Once you know the problem you can help them take care of it. So, learn to listen to what your young child needs. Get to know your baby's cries or your toddler's whines.

Getting Your Child to Come When You Call (Transitions)

Parents hate it when children do not come when they are called. For example, pretend your child is playing with his toys. You say, "It is time for dinner. Come to the table." But your child does not move. He pretends he does not hear you. Or maybe he is so interested in what he is doing that he really does not hear you. So you get angry and say, "Come to the table, now!" But your child still does not move. Now both of you are angry and upset.

You may think your child is misbehaving. That may be true. But there is something else that is happening, too. When children start doing something, they have a hard time stopping. We want them to stop when we say stop. If they do not stop, we may get angry. But they are not trying to make us angry. They just need some time to change what they are doing. They need some time to finish their play and change to something else. When we talk about this problem, we say,

"Children have lousy brakes."

They take a long time to slow down and stop. You can help your child by giving her time to get ready to stop her play. This helps her learn to make a transition from one thing to another.

For example, you can say, "Dinner will be ready soon. You have only a few minutes to finish what you are doing."

Then wait three or four minutes and say, "Dinner is almost ready. Please stop what you are doing. Come and wash your hands."

Some parents say, "OK. You have 2 minutes to stop. Then you need to wash your hands for dinner."

Remember that your young child cannot tell time. But when you try this method, he will learn how long 2 minutes is very quickly. Some children like it when you use a timer. Set the timer for 5 or 10 minutes. Tell them that they will need to stop when the timer rings. For example, say, "I am setting the timer for 5 minutes. Try to put your socks and shoes on before it rings."

Some parents let their children have "one more time" before they have to stop. Example: "You can go down the slide one more time. Then we go home."

Be careful to do what you say. "One more time" means one time and not ten times. Use this way to teach your child how to slow down, and she will behave better and better.

The Beauty of a Good Rule

Often children misbehave because they do not know how to act. They need to learn. And they will learn if we teach them the right way. Making rules is one way to teach them. When they follow the rules, they learn how to get along with others. Making good rules will help you prevent many problems. Then, as your children grow up, they will know how to act their best.

Why do we make rules?

1. **We have rules to protect children.** Children do not know that the world can be dangerous. We make rules to keep them safe. Children also don't know how dangerous they can be. So we often have to set rules to keep them from hurting themselves, other children, pets, or objects in the house. For example:

   Rule: Children do not play with knives.

   Rule: We wear a coat when it is cold outside.

Rule: We do not bite people.

Rule: We do not hit people.

2. **We have rules to keep children from having to make choices they're not ready for.** They do not have the experience yet to make all of their choices. Rules help them when they are not old enough to make good decisions. For example:

> **Rule:** Children can watch only the movies parents choose. (They are not ready to watch all movies. Some are too scary, violent or include scenes inappropriate for kids.)

> **Rule:** We eat sweets only after we eat our dinner. (It is not healthy for children to eat sweets instead of healthy food. In fact you may decide not to let your young child eat sweets at all, or only rarely.)

3. **We have rules to get children ready for life in a world of rules.** Since we live in a world where everyone has rules and laws, we want to help our children learn that it's usually best to follow the rules. Starting life with this idea can help children get along better with others and avoid many problems later. For example:

> **Rule:** We take turns on the swing.

> **Rule:** We put the blocks in the box when we are finished playing.

4. **We have rules to make parenting easier.** When you set clear rules in your home and make sure everyone follows them all the time, then you won't have to work as hard at discipline. When children know what kind of behavior you expect from them, they are less likely to misbehave. You should not have to think of what to do each time something happens. Instead, you can apply a rule. Plus, if your child knows your rules, he will misbehave less. For example:

> **Rule:** We do not eat food in the bedroom.

> **Rule:** Dirty clothes go in the hamper.

Tips for Making Rules

1. **Make only the rules you really need.** It is hard for young children to remember a lot of rules. Older children can remember more. At first, rules about health and safety are the most important. You might wait until your child is 4 or 5 years old before you teach rules about manners.

   Children can understand the idea of fairness very early, so be sure that you have a good reason for every rule you make. For example, "We brush our teeth every night so that they will be clean and healthy." Even if your child is too young to fully understand the reason, it helps her learn that it's important to have good reasons for what you do.

2. **Give one rule at a time.** Keep it Simple and Short (KISS). Remember, your child's brain is not as developed as yours yet. It's easier for her to follow just one rule at a time.

3. **Try to leave the child out of the rule.** For example, say, "Bedtime is at 8:00," not "You have to go to bed at 8:00." The first way, with the child out of the rule, sounds more like a rule that should be followed all the time, not like something you want your child to do then and only then. And once a rule becomes a habit, it will be a lot easier for both you and your child.

4. **Say the rule in a positive way.** When some children hear "Don't," they take it as a challenge to do it. Instead of saying, "Don't jump on the sofa," try saying, "Sofas are for sitting on. Please sit down."

5. **Say it like you mean it.** Stand close to your child and, if possible, get down to her eye-level. Use a firm, calm voice.

6. **Be consistent in enforcing the rule.** If you sometimes remind your child when he is breaking a rule, but sometimes ignore him, he will think that your rules don't really matter. Be consistent, and he will learn that the rule is important and you mean what you say.

7. **Encourage your child when he remembers a rule.** Give him a smile or a hug. Show him you know he is acting responsibly. Soon he will feel good about your rules.

✏✏✏ Making Rules Worksheet ✏✏✏

Think of a problem you are having with your child and write it below.

Problem:_____

Now write a rule for this problem.

Rule:_____

Next, check your rule with these questions:

- ■ Do you really need this rule? Do you have good reason for it?
- ■ Is the rule short and simple?
- ■ Did you leave the child out of the rule?
- ■ Is the rule positive?

The next time your child misbehaves, tell him the rule. Afterwards, answer these questions.

Did you say the rule in a firm and calm voice? _____

Did your child obey the rule? _____
_____

If "yes," did you encourage her? How? _____
_____

If "no," did you do what you said you would do if he broke the rule?
_____
_____

Then what happened?
_____
_____
_____

Discipline Skill: The When-Then Rule

Remember that discipline means to teach. This rule will help you teach your child to do something that she does not want to do. Here is how it works. You tell your child that **when** she does what you want her to do, **then** she can do what she wants to do.

For example, Isabel does not like to take a bath. She says "no" every night. But she does like her Mom to read her a story. So Isabel's mother says, "Isabel, **when** you take your bath, **then** I will read you a story." She chooses to take a bath because she wants to hear a story. That is the When-Then rule.

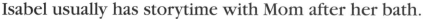

When-Then Rule Tips

When you use this rule remember:

1. **Do not give a special reward for the choice.** What your child gets to do should be something she usually does and likes. For example, Isabel usually has storytime with Mom after her bath.

   If you give a special reward, such as toys or candy or staying up late, your child will always expect it. This will cause problems later.

2. **Always say "When..., then...."** For example:
   - "**When** you put all your cars in the box, **then** we can go get a snack."
   - "**When** you get your coat on, **then** we can go to the park."

3. **Be firm and friendly when you use the rule.** If your voice is "too hard" or "too soft," the rule will not work as well.

4. **Look at your child when you talk to her.** You may need to get on the floor to be close to her. Your eye-to-eye contact gets your child's attention. It also lets her know you mean what you say.

✎ ✐ When-Then Rule Worksheet ✐ ✎

Are you having a problem with your child? Do you have a hard time getting her to do something? Write that under "My Problem" below:

Example: Ben does not like to get into bed at night.

My Problem:

_____

_____

_____

What will you say to your child the next time you have this problem with him or her? Think of what your child likes to do. Write it under "My When-Then Rule" below.

Example:

   "**When** you have gotten into bed,

   then you can choose a book for me to read to you."

My When-Then Rule:

   When_____

   Then_____

Try this at home with your child. After you try it, write down what happened here:

_____

_____

_____

_____

_____

_____

_____

_____

Can you use When-Then rules with babies?

Yes. Remember that discipline means to teach. When you talk to your baby you are teaching her language. So, it is a good idea to tell her what you are doing and why…even before she can understand you. This can apply to anything you do with your baby, including when-then actions. For example:

"When I've taken off your wet diaper,
then I'll put on a dry one."

"When I've finished drying you off,
then you can have your bottle."

Although you are doing the action instead of getting the child to do it, a When-Then rule like this can help her begin learning how the steps work.

■ ■ ■ ■ ■ ■ ■ ■ ■ ■ ■ ■ ■ ■ ■ ■

Discipline Skill: The ACT Method[2]

The When-Then rule is great for getting your child to start doing something. But how do you teach your child to stop doing something? For example:

"How can I teach Tanya not to jump on the bed?"

You can use the ACT method. It has 3 steps:

Step 1: Accept your child's wishes or feelings.

Tell her it is OK for her to want something. Let her know you understand how she feels. This does not mean you give her what she wants. It means you understand her feelings. Here is an example of Step 1, accepting your child's wishes or feelings:

"Tanya, I know you like to bounce and jump."

Step 2: Communicate the rule.

Tell your child the rules. Let her know that you understand how she feels, but you do not like how she acts. Be calm when you speak to her. Tell her that the way she is acting is not OK. Tell her the right way to act. Here is an example of Step 2, communicating the rule:

> *"But beds are for sleeping, not jumping.*
> *You might fall off and get hurt."*

Step 3: Target a positive choice.

After you tell your child what she cannot do, give her another choice. Give her something else she can do. Help her find a better way to get her wish. Here is an example of Step 3, targeting a positive choice:

> *"We can line up some pillows on the floor*
> *for you to jump on, like this!"*

Young children are easy to distract. They may stop what they are doing if there is something new to do. They like new things and are quick to move on.

Let's look at some more examples of a parent using the ACT method.

Example:

Step 1: Accept your child's wishes or feelings.	*"Maggie, I'm glad you like to play basketball. It looks like you are having fun."*
Step 2: Communicate the rule.	*"But we do not play basketball inside our home."*
Step 3: Target a positive choice.	*"I will take you outside later. Right now we can set up a little hoop in your room. You can use the foam ball Uncle Wilt gave you to play in the house."*

72

Here is another example:

Step 1:	**A**ccept your child's wishes or feelings.	*"I know you are angry with me."*
Step 2:	**C**ommunicate the rule.	*"But we do not scream at each other."*
Step 3:	**T**arget a positive choice.	*"You can go scream in your room. When you feel calmer, we can talk about what is upsetting you."*

Sometimes you do not have time to think of the steps in the right order.

For example, Pete, a two-year-old, is chewing on a balloon. His dad remembers that many children die when balloons get caught in their throats. So he needs to act fast. He takes the balloon out of Pete's mouth and says, "No. We do not put balloons in our mouths. They can pop and get caught in your throat. I know you like to taste things. But balloons are not safe for you. Let me put this away. I will get you a cracker that you can eat."

Pete's father used the ACT method and said all the steps. He just said them in a different order. That's OK if something dangerous is about to happen. At other times, try to use the steps in the A-C-T order.

ACT Method Tips

Children watch what we do more than what we say. Do you do what you say you will do? If you do, then your child will learn to listen to you. Here are three things that will help you when you use the ACT method:

1. **Look your child in the eyes when you talk to him.** You may need to get on your knees to look at him. Or you may need to hold him on your lap and look at his face. When you talk to him this way, he will hear you better.

2. **Show your child another choice.** For example, if Pete sees the cracker, he will give Dad the balloon. If Maggie sees the foam ball, she will give up the hard ball.

3. **You may have to move the child.** If your child does not stop what she is doing, what do you do? You should move her. You can do this by gently lifting under her arms. Point her in another direction. If she will not move, stay calm and gentle. Give her a choice.

For example, ask, "Do you want to walk by yourself or do you want me to carry you?"

If she does not move on her own, pick her up and say, "I guess you want me to carry you."

If she screams and cries, take her to her room or to another quiet place. Tell her when she stops crying and yelling, then she can come out and play. After two to four minutes, ask her if she is ready to stop crying and come out. If she says yes, give her a hug. But if she still cries, tell her you will come back later. Check again in two to four minutes, and then every five to ten minutes. (There is more about tantrums in Chapter 3.)

✏ ✏ ✏ ACT Method Worksheet ✏ ✏ ✏

Think of a problem you are having with your child—something that your child does that you want him or her to stop doing. Write it below.

Problem #1:_____

_____

Now write what you will say for each of the 3 steps of the ACT method:

Step 1: A (Accept your child's wishes or feelings.)

"I know you like to" or "I know you feel _____

_____

_____ "

Step 2: C (Communicate the rule.)

"But _____

_____ "

Step 3: T (Target a positive choice.)

"How about _____ "

■ ■ ■ ■ ■ ■ ■ ■ ■ ■ ■ ■ ■ ■

Problem #2_____

_____

Step 1: A "_____

_____ "

Step 2: C "_____

_____ "

Step 3: T "_____

_____ "

What happened when you tried this at home with your child? _____

_____

Building the Bond: Routines

Do you do some things each day at about the same time and in the same order? This is called a routine. Children love routines! They love to do the same things the same way over and over. They want to know that some things will happen again and again. Routines help children feel safe and secure. They also make those brain connections stronger. Here are some routines that may help you:

Morning routine:

- Do your children wake up the same time each morning?

- Do they wash, brush their teeth, and get dressed in the same order?

- Do they eat breakfast at the same time each morning?

Eating routine:

- Do they eat lunch and dinner at about the same time each day?

- Do they eat in the same place each day?

Sleeping routine:

- Do they take a nap each day?

- Do they take a nap the same time each day?

- Do they do the same things each night before they go to bed?

- Do they go to bed at the same time each night?

A routine will help your child learn how to act, and it will teach your child the rules. It will also help your child feel secure. If you make the routines fun, your child will learn to enjoy them. (Remember, you can change a routine if another one is better. You can also make exceptions to a routine when you need to.)

76

✐ ✐ ✐ Routines Worksheet ✐ ✐ ✐

Here are some examples of routines used by parents (or other caregivers):

MORNING ROUTINE

6:00   Parent wakes up. Parent gets herself ready.

6:30   Parent wakes up Jenny, her three-year-old and gently kisses jenny on the cheek. She says, "Time to get up, JenJen."

6:31   Parent turns on a lamp. She takes some clothes out of the closet. She says, "Jenny, do you want to wear this red shirt or that blue shirt?"

6:35   Parent helps Jenny get dressed. She lets Jenny do as much as she can by herself.

6:45   Parent makes breakfast. Parent asks Jenny what kind of cereal she wants that day. Then Parent pours juice for them both.

7:05   Parent takes Jenny to the bathroom. Parent helps her brush her teeth and wash her face. Parent brushes her hair.

7:15   Parent and Jenny get in the car. Parent drives to childcare.

Write a morning routine that you can use with your child.

Time   Activity

_____   _____

_____   _____

_____   _____

_____   _____

_____   _____

_____   _____

_____   _____

_____   _____

NAPTIME ROUTINE (FOR NAPS DURING THE DAY)

2:00   Parent and Joey, a two-year-old, get in a rocking chair to read a story.

2:15   The story is finished. Parent plays soft music or sings softly to Joey. Parent rocks him.

2:20   Parent puts Joey in the bed. Parent says, "Sleep well, sweetheart. I love you."

4:00   Joey wakes up and calls for his Parent. Parent comes into the bedroom and says, "Did you have a good nap?" Parent picks him up and says, "Would you like some juice?" They go to the kitchen and have some juice.

Write a naptime routine that you can use with your child.

Time   Activity

_____   _____

_____   _____

_____   _____

_____   _____

_____   _____

_____   _____

_____   _____

_____   _____

_____   _____

BEDTIME ROUTINE

7:30   Parent fills the bathtub. Parent tells Daniel, his four-year-old, to take his clothes off.

7:35   Parent gives Daniel a bath. Parent plays some fun music and puts two or three toys in the bathtub for Daniel. Parent plays with Daniel before starting to bathe him. (Note: Never leave a young child alone in the bathtub. He may drown!)

7:45   Parent dries Daniel and helps him put on his pajamas. Parent helps son brush his teeth and comb his hair.

7:55   Parent reads Daniel a story.

8:05   Parent and son say a prayer. Parent says, "I love you, son." Daniel says, "I love you, too." Parent turns off the light and leaves the door open a little. (Note: Your child should sleep in his own bed, if possible. If he gets scared at night and gets in your bed, take him back to his bed, comfort him, and stay for a little while before saying, Goodnight.")

Write a bedtime routine that you can use with your child:

Time   Activity

_____ _____

_____ _____

_____ _____

_____ _____

_____ _____

_____ _____

_____ _____

_____ _____

_____ _____

_____ _____

The Importance of Sleep

Scientists are really just beginning to understand the many ways that sleep is essential to healthy living for children…and for adults. For example, sleep plays a part in:

- Physical and mental health
- Cell repair
- Brain development
- Attention span and ability to focus
- Behavior
- Learning ability

We also know that too little sleep is especially bad for children. And though each child is a little difference, here are some guidelines endorsed by the American Academy of Pediatrics that can give you an idea about how much sleep a young child needs at different ages.

Hours of Sleep Recommended per Day (including naps) on a Regular Basis[3]

Infants 4 to 12 months:	12 to 16 hours
Children 1 to 2 years:	11 to 14 hours
Children 3 to 5 years:	10 to 13 hours

If you do not think that your child is getting enough sleep, a good bedtime routine can help. But if you still see a problem, be sure to consult with your child's pediatrician to check for other possible sources of the problem. See page 53 for important information about sleep safety for babies.

Building the Bond: Hugs, Kisses, and 3 Little Words

All children need lots of loving touch. In fact, without it they will not thrive. So it is a good thing that nature made parents like to hold, kiss, and stroke their children, too. We now know that there is a hormone called *oxytocin* that is released in both children and parents when they share love and affection. It makes us both feel good at these times. It also bonds us together.

---

3   From the American Academy of Sleep Medicine (AASM). The American Academy of Pediatrics (AAP) has issued a Statement of Endorsement supporting the AASM.

When you say the words "I love you" while you lovingly touch your child, she learns to feel good when she hears these words. Your child needs to hear those words from you often. Tell your child you love him every day. Hug him and kiss him each day, too. Many times. Tell him when he takes a nap. Tell him before he goes to bed at night. Tell him many times during the day. Watch him smile when he hears the words. You cannot give your child too much love. You cannot spoil your child with love, either.

■ ■

SPECIAL NEEDS

It is especially important to say "I love you" to a child who is going through a challenging period or has special needs. Their courage and self-esteem may be low. Knowing that their parents love them and are glad to have them can help give them the confidence to deal with problems. They need to know that their parents love them just as they are and that "just as they are," they are lovable.

✏ ✏ ✏ "I Love You" Worksheet ✏ ✏ ✏

When did you say "I love you" to your child this week? _____
_____
_____

How did you lovingly touch your child when you said it? _____
_____
_____

Where were you? _____
_____

What did your child say? _____
_____

How did you feel? _____
_____

Taking Care of Yourself Worksheet

Remember that an important part of parenting "just right" is taking good care of yourself. Turn back to your list of self-care ideas on page 39. Add any new ideas you have learned. Then choose two ideas to do this week and write them below. After you do each activity, answer the questions about it.

Self-care activity #1:

_____

_____

_____

Self-care activity #2:

_____

_____

_____

After self-care activity #1 I felt:

_____

_____

After self-care activity #2 I felt:

_____

_____

How did these activities help you be a better parent?

_____

_____

_____

_____

_____

_____

82

Home Activities

Check the box beside each activity after you complete it this week:

- ☐ I will use a When-Then rule with my child.

- ☐ I will use the ACT method with my child.

- ☐ I will create a bedtime routine for my child that includes both words ("I love you") and touch (hugs and kisses).

- ☐ I will read Chapter 2 and complete the activities.

- ☐ I will practice mindfulness this week and teach my child how to do the exercises, too (if appropriate for his or her age).

- ☐ I will continue taking time every day to play with my child (For example, "Freeze Dance," if it is age-appropriate).

Do these 6 things at home this week, then answer these questions:

This is what happened when I used a When-Then rule with my child:

_____

_____

_____

This is what happened when I used the ACT method with my child:

_____

_____

_____

This is what happened when I created a bedtime routine for my child:

_____

_____

_____

After I practiced mindfulness, I felt: _____

_____

After I played with my child, I felt: _____

_____

CHAPTER 3

Encouraging Positive Behavior

Temperament and Discipline

In Chapter 1 we talked about how all young children are both the same and different. They are the same because they all go through the same stages of development from the "Baby" stage to the "Adventurer" stage. They are different because they each come into the world with their own personality or "temperament."

Think back to when you were growing up. Did you live with a brother or sister? Did you act like your brother or sister? No. You acted like you. Every child has a different temperament. Every parent has a different temperament, too.

This chapter is about helping your child learn how to behave in positive ways. Before you can do that, it helps to know your child's temperament. That will give you an idea of where your child needs help and where he is doing OK on his own.

All of these temperaments are normal. They all have benefits, too. For example, does your child have high energy and a strong will? This child may be what we call "spirited." That may mean she is hard to live with sometimes. But she may also use these same traits to become a leader when she grows up.

Or does your child have low energy? He probably acts cranky when he has to do many things in one day. But he also may like to play by himself quietly when he can.

You can help your child work with his or her temperament. But first you will need to learn more about it. The Temperament Checklist on the next page will guide you through some questions that will reveal more about your child's temperament. If you have more than one child, choose one of them for this exercise and write it in the blank at the top of the page.

Temperament Checklist

Child's name: _____

What is her energy level?

- ☐ High energy
- ☐ Medium energy
- ☐ Low energy

How does she feel about change?

- ☐ Likes changes
- ☐ Can accept changes
- ☐ Does not like changes

How does she feel about other people?

- ☐ Enjoys people and likes to play with other children
- ☐ Sometimes enjoys people; sometimes likes to play by herself
- ☐ Likes to play by herself

What are your child's feelings?

- ☐ Usually happy, pleasant
- ☐ Is sometimes happy, sometimes sad
- ☐ Often either unhappy or sad

What is your child's will-power like?

- ☐ Strong-willed; likes to lead
- ☐ Medium-willed
- ☐ Gentle; likes to follow

How is your child organized?

- ☐ Likes to be very neat
- ☐ Is neat sometimes
- ☐ Is usually messy

86

Temperament Tips

After you complete the Temperament Checklist, read how you can help your child work with each of her traits.

☐ **Has high energy:**

This child needs a lot of OK ways to use her energy. Take her to the playground or some place where she can run and jump and make noise. Give her pots and pans or toys she can swing, throw, or kick.

☐ **Has low energy:**

This child may get tired easily. Let her play quietly. She can read, draw pictures, or watch movies. You can slowly help her play with more energy as she grows.

☐ **Likes changes:**

This child enjoys going from one activity to another. He likes to go to new places and try new things. Help him also learn to stick with an activity for a little longer.

☐ **Does not like changes:**

This child likes to stick with daily routines. Help her learn to try new things. Do not force her, but encourage her to explore.

☐ **Enjoys people:**

This child will be very friendly to other people. He may want to talk to strangers. You should watch him closely, since some strangers may be harmful.

☐ **Likes to play by himself:**

This child is shy. But she will talk to people when she knows them. Tell your child about new people before she meets them. Help her play with others.

Continued on next page.

☐ Is happy, pleasant:

This child may be easy to live with as he is. Enjoy him. But also look for the unpleasant feelings he may sometimes have but not show.

☐ Is often unhappy or sad:

Help this child look at the happy side of life. Point out the good things that happen, even when these things are small!

☐ Has a strong will; likes to lead:

Give this child lots of times to be the boss. Also give her choices to make instead of orders to take. Help her cooperate with others.

☐ Is gentle; likes to follow:

This child may be kind to others. You might need to help him be stronger. For example, if someone takes his toy, teach him how to ask for it.

☐ Likes to be very neat:

Teach this child how to relax and enjoy life. She does not need to always have everything neat and in place.

☐ Is usually messy:

Help your child to be neater. Teach him to pick up toys and put away clothes.

✏ ✏ ✏ Temperament Worksheet ✏ ✏ ✏

Put an **X** where you are. Put a ☐ where your child is. For example, if most of the time you have high energy, and your child has low energy, you would mark the chart like this:

Low energy ————————**X**————☐———— High energy

Likes change ————————————————— Does not like change

Likes people and
playing with them ————————————————— Likes to play
by himself

Happy mood ————————————————— Unhappy mood

Likes to lead ————————————————— Likes to follow

Neat ————————————————— Messy

1. When are the **X**s and the ☐s in the same spots? These are areas where you and your child probably get along best.

    _____

    _____

2. When are the **X**s and the ☐s in different spots? These are areas where you and your child may have a hard time understanding each other. List these areas:

    _____

    _____

3. Which of your own traits will you work to improve?

    _____

    _____

4. How will you help your child improve some of his traits?

    _____

    _____

Discipline Skill: Choices and Consequences

We want to help our children learn how to behave in positive ways. This may mean helping a child who has lots of energy learn not to run inside your home. Or, it may mean helping a child who does not follow rules to learn to follow them. It may mean taking the time to teach a child respect and how to be polite. But how do you do all of this?

We can use many of the methods from Chapter 2. For example, we can make good rules and use the When-Then rule and the ACT method. Even so, children will still misbehave sometimes.

When your child misbehaves, you may feel like yelling, hitting, or shaking him. But this can be very harmful to your child, and it is not good for you, either. So instead, take some deep breaths and calm yourself. Then use a non-violent discipline skill that teaches instead of hurts your child. It is called **choices and consequences**.

Each time we make a choice, something happens. The things that happen are called consequences. Your child will learn that each time she makes a **choice**, there will be a **consequence**.

Remember the ACT method? Look at this example of a two-year-old who hits his mother:

Step 1: **A**ccept your child's wishes or feelings.

"Son, I know you feel angry."

Step 2: **C**ommunicate the rule.

"But in our family, we do not hit people."

Step 3: **T**arget a positive choice.

"How about hitting this pillow to show how mad you are?"

90

What happens if your son says, "No!" and hits you again? You can give him a choice. The child can choose to <u>be angry without hitting</u>, or he can choose for you to do something that will help him learn how to behave. The second choice is the **consequence.** For example:

*"You can **either** <u>stay here without hitting me</u> **or** <u>you can go to the bedroom to hit your pillow.</u> It is your choice."*

This is sometimes called an "Either-Or" choice, because it uses the words "either" and "or" to separate the two choices. Once children are through with the Baby stage (about age one) they can learn to recognize and respond to Either-Or choices.

If the child in our example stops hitting, then he chose to behave. But if he hits you again, that means he chose the **consequence.** Then you gently tell him the **consequence.** You say, "I see you chose to go to the bedroom. Tell me when you are ready to come out and stay here without hitting." You take him by the hand and lead him to the bedroom.

What if your child hits again later? That is his choice. He will have the same **consequence.** Each time he hits you, you will take him to the bedroom. If you are in another place, take him away from the person he was hitting. He needs to learn that each time he hits there will be a consequence. The consequence is that he gets removed from the situation. Note: Do not hit him to punish him. You are trying to teach him not to hit, so you should not hit either.

Tips for Using Consequences

1. Consequences should make sense. The consequence you choose should be logically connected to the child's misbehavior. In fact, this method is sometimes called "logical consequences." This helps the child learn that he has some power over the consequences that happen to him. This is a great way to begin teaching your child responsibility. The child who learns, "I am responsible for my choices" has a very good chance of learning from his mistakes and making better choices in the future. You use a consequence to teach your child how to act. You do not use it to punish or hurt your child.

EXAMPLE 1:

Your child is playing a game of cards with you. He keeps throwing the cards around the room. You can give him a choice.

Good choice:

*"You can either stop throwing the cards
or you will have to stop playing the game."*

Hurtful choice:

*"You can either stop throwing the cards
or you will get a spanking."*

If he has to stop playing as a consequence of him throwing the cards, he will learn not to throw the cards. But if you spank him, he will just get mad. Spanking will only hurt him. Spanking will not teach him to stop throwing the cards because it does not fit the situation. It does not make sense to the child.

EXAMPLE 2:

Your child keeps wandering off while you are shopping at the grocery store. You can give her a choice.

Good choice:

*"Either stay with me or you will need to ride
in the cart. You decide."*

Hurtful choice:

"Either stay with me or you cannot watch TV tonight."

92

Think about the misbehavior. In this case, it is not staying with you at the grocery store. Consequences work best when they fit the misbehavior. Having your child ride in the cart fits because she cannot go off on her own if she is in the cart. Keeping her from watching TV does not fit. Children learn best when the consequence fits. Again, we call this a "logical consequence."

EXAMPLE 3:

You tell your child to put away his blocks. He does not listen to you. You can give him a choice:

Good choice:

> *"Either put your blocks away or I will put them in a box in the closet."*

Hurtful choice:

> *"Either put your blocks away or you will have to stand in the corner for five minutes."*

Not getting to play with the blocks fits the misbehavior. It teaches the child to take care of his things. It is a logical consequence. Standing in the corner does not fit. It has nothing to do with the blocks.

2. **Keep your tone of voice firm and calm.** If you yell or are angry, he will only know you are mad. Then he may do it again to see if you get mad again. If you use a firm and calm voice, he will listen to your words. This is the way to teach your child about consequences.

3. **Give only choices and consequences that are OK with you.** You are the parent. You have a right to limit your child's choices to ones that you approve.

For example, Mother tells her two-year-old son, Stephen, "Either stop biting or I will have to hold you so you cannot bite." Stephen tries to bite again, and Mother gets angry. She says, "I don't have time for this, Stephen!" Then she spanks him.

The mother gave her child a choice that was not OK with her. When her son chose to bite again, she got mad. She did not do what she said she would do. That teaches her son not to trust her choices.

Here is a better choice the mother could have used:

"Either play without biting or play alone in your crib, Stephen."

4. **Give the choice one time. Then act!** It is how you act that will teach your child. What happens when you give a choice and do not act? Your child learns to not listen to you. What happens when you give a choice one time and act? Your child learns to listen to what you say.

    For example, Caleb and Emily like to play together. But sometimes one of them will hit the other. Father says, "Either play together without hitting, or you will each have to play alone in separate rooms." The next time one of the children hits the other while playing, Father sends them to separate rooms for ten minutes. After a few tries, Caleb and Emily learn to play together without hitting.

    (Note: At another time, Father should teach his children how to solve problems peacefully. But for now, putting them in separate rooms without blaming one or the other is a good consequence.)

Children with special needs can benefit from choices and consequences, too. But be aware that depending on your child's special needs, it may take more time for them to learn from the consequences of their choices. So, be prepared to be patient. And practice your own self-calming methods so that you don't get frustrated.

Choices & Consequences Worksheet

Are you having a problem with your child? Write it in this space:

Problem: _____

Write a choice and a consequence for your child as an **Either-Or** choice:

Either _____

_____

or _____

_____

Or you can write it this way, using the **When-Then** rule:

When _____

_____

then _____

_____

Use this choice and consequence the next time you have this problem with your child. After you do it, fill in these blanks:

What happened? _____

_____

_____

Was your voice firm and calm? _____

Did your child listen to you the first time? _____

Will you change how you act the next time? _____

Brain-Building Activity: Panda & Frog

Last chapter we learned some games that strengthen the skill of being able to stop and consider our thoughts before acting. Children need to learn this skill to make good decisions. We are going to continue working on it with a game called Panda and Frog.

For this game, use the Panda and Frog pictures on pages 97-99. You can play this game with one or more children. The rules for children are simple:

<u>Do</u> what Panda says. <u>Do not do</u> what Frog says.

To lead the game, call out a series of directions: either "Panda says, _____" or "Frog says, _____." Hold up the matching picture as you give each direction.

Start with several Panda commands. For example:

> "Panda says touch your ear."

> "Panda says rub your belly."

> "Panda says clap your hands."

Start mixing in an occasional Frog command. For example:

> "Panda says stick out your tongue."

> "Panda says stamp your left foot."

> "Frog says touch your nose."

> "Panda says stand on your right foot."

> "Frog says wave your right hand."

If the participants are doing well following the directions, you can start mixing in more Frog commands to make it more difficult.

AGE GUIDELINES: This game is appropriate for children age one and older. For the youngest, use only Panda commands. As age increases or as children master the Panda commands, add Frog commands until there is an even mix of Panda and Frog.

If older children (age 4-5) need a greater challenge after they have played the game for a while, try changing the rules: "<u>Do</u> what *Frog* says. <u>Do not do</u> what *Panda* says." Start with mostly Frog commands, then begin to add Panda commands. As children master this game, change the rules more often to add more challenge.

Panda

Frog

Can you discipline a baby?

No. Babies are too young for discipline. Their brains have not developed enough yet for them to understand the relationship between choices and consequences. Efforts to discipline them will just frustrate them—and you even more.

Focus on learning what soothes your baby, not on trying to correct his behavior. Keep him away from dangerous things since you can't teach him how to avoid danger himself yet. If your baby wants something he shouldn't have, like a marble that he wants to put in his mouth, try using the ACT method to redirect him to something else. Or move him. Or remove the thing he wants. And never ever <u>ever</u> shake, hit, or spank your baby.

What should you do if you are getting too frustrated or angry with a crying baby or young child and feel that you might hurt him? Here are some tips for self-calming in this situation:

- Have someone you can call, like a relative, a friend, or a neighbor, to take over for a little while so you can have a break. Use the time to take a walk or do something else away from your child that relaxes you.

- If you don't have someone to call, put your baby or child in a safe place (crib, play pen, their room) and take a short break away from him. Use your self-calming techniques to calm yourself before returning to your child.

- Remind yourself that you love and support your child.

- If you don't have anyone to help and you are close to your wits' end, you can reach out for help from a doctor or other professional or a crisis hotline. Keep a list of important contact numbers handy. (See "Where You Can Go for Help" on page 113 for more information.)

- Join a Moms'/Dads' Club or parenting class. Other parents can be a great source of information, comfort, and companionship.

- REMEMBER: Never shake, hit, or spank your baby or young child. You might cause serious, lasting damage to their brains, their bodies, or your relationship with each other.

Tantrums

When your young child wants something he cannot have, or wants to do something he can not do, or just feels bad and does not know how to feel better, he may get **frustrated**. This feeling of frustration can become **anger**. Young children do not have much experience handling anger. They may yell and cry. They may even throw things or fall on the floor and kick. This is called a **tantrum**. Many children have tantrums. It is their way of expressing their anger. Sometimes it also becomes a way of getting what they want. Here's how it works:

Babies cry when they are hurting or need something. It is good for parents to respond to their cries and give them what they want. But as babies grow into toddlers , we need to start teaching them how to take care of some of their own needs. They also need to begin learning how to manage their own frustrations.

Example: A child has a tantrum because she can't have something she wants. Her parents get frustrated with her crying and give her what she wants. What do you think the child learns? She probably learns that tantrums are a good way to get what she wants. She learns to use her anger or "temper" to get what she wants.

NOT GETTING WHAT YOU WANT

↓

FRUSTRATION

↓

ANGER or TEMPER

↓

TEMPER TANTRUMS

↓

VIOLENCE

100

We want to avoid sending the message to our children that it's OK to use their temper and violence to get their way. We want to teach them better ways to handle problems.

Your child learns from what you do more than from what you say. So, if you want to teach your child to solve problems without violence, you have to set a good example. That means managing your own anger without violence. It means using non-violent discipline skills with your child. And it means teaching your child ways to manage anger in positive ways instead of having a tantrum. For example:

- Use a self-calming method such as the mindfulness methods in this book or taking deep breaths.

- Solve the problem. He might be able to find a good way to get what he wants.

- Accept that sometimes you don't get what you want. Show him he can replace anger with acceptance.

- Find an alternative. Remember step 3 in the ACT method: Target a positive alternative.

These are not easy lessons to learn, especially for young children. So, be patient. This is the time to begin teaching your child to manage emotions and solve problems. But it may take a year or more with some children.

Tips for Handling Tantrums

1. **Stay calm.** If you get angry, your child will learn to do the same thing. Stay calm and think about what is happening.

2. **Help your child to get calm.** There are many ways to help a child calm down and to learn how to calm themselves down. Learn what works best for your child. For example:

   - **Step back from her.** If your child is not a danger to herself or others, step back and let her finish. Don't ignore her, but don't participate, either. We call this "taking your sail out of your child's wind." It means you don't fight or give in. You can say, "I cannot talk to you when you are crying and screaming. When you are finished, we will talk about it."

- **Talk gently.** Stay close and talk "low and slow." Be soothing and understanding. You can say, "It's OK. I know. You will be all right. I am here."

- **Hold her gently (while you talk gently).** Hold her with gentle arms until she is quiet. **Important:** This will work only if you hug and hold your child when she is happy, too. Do you hold her only when she has a tantrum? Then she will have a tantrum when she wants your love or hugs.

If the child is a danger to herself or others, you can restrain her firmly but still gently (not roughly) with your arms. Hold her and talk "low and slow." You can say,

"It's okay, just take some deep breaths."

"When you calm yourself down, we can talk about how to get what you want."

"I don't want you to hurt yourself, so when you calm yourself down I can let you go."

3. **Do not give your child what she wants to get her to stop yelling and screaming.** She will learn to have a tantrum to get her way. Wait until she has finished or help him calm down. Remember Step 3 of the ACT method: Target a positive choice. You can say, "You cannot have a cookie now. It is almost time for dinner. You can have a cracker or some cheese."

4. **Give a choice and a consequence.** When possible, let your child have her tantrum where she is. Walk away from her but stay nearby so you can make sure she stays safe.

But sometimes you cannot just let it happen. Your child may have a tantrum in front of other people. In that situation, give your child a

102

choice. Say to your child, "Either take some deep breaths and calm down, or you can scream in your room." If she chooses not to try to calm down, you can gently carry her to her room. If you are in a store, take her outside until she is calm. If you have a car, put her in the car seat and sit quietly in your seat. Wait a few minutes. Then ask her, "Are you ready to be calm and go back inside?" Most children will be calm now. If she is not calm, wait a few minutes. Then ask her again.

 Some children with special needs or a "spirited" temperament have more extreme tantrums. It is more like a "meltdown." Their brains become flooded with emotion and they can't think clearly. These meltdowns can last hours unless someone helps the child calm down. If this sounds like your child, keep two things in mind:

1. If you can learn what triggers these tantrums, you can take steps to prevent them.

2. Teach your child how to self-calm with mindfulness exercises. The best time to do this is when your child is already calm.

(For more help with spirited children, read Dr. Popkin's book Taming the Spirited Child, *available from www.ActiveParenting.com or Amazon.)*

Tips for Avoiding Tantrums

1. **Make sure your child gets plenty of sleep.** If she is tired, she will have tantrums more often. For example, is your child tired when you bring her shopping with you? Be sure she has a nap before you go out.

2. **Make sure your child eats healthy food.** Often children have tantrums when they are thirsty or hungry. So pack a healthy snack when you go out together. Some children are sensitive to sugar or other foods. Pay attention to how your child reacts to different foods and cut out or reduce the ones that cause problems.

3. **Let your child do things with you.** Your child is interested in many things. If you go to the store, let her help you. She can put food in the cart. Talk to her, ask her questions, or give her something to do while you shop.

4. **Find things your child can do at home.** Find things she can do for herself that are not too hard. If she is too young to button a shirt, get big buttons for her or something that snaps.

5. **When your child goes out with you, bring along something fun.** Bring a coloring book and crayons or some small toys. Sing songs together while you are waiting. Play games together.

6. **Use the ACT method to help her find other good things to do.** If she wants something she cannot have, help her find a choice she can have BEFORE she has a tantrum.

7. **Take some deep breaths together.** When you see her beginning to "lose it," you can say, "I'm starting to feel frustrated. I think I need to take some deep breaths and calm down. Will you help me?" This puts the two of you "in the same boat" so it will be easier for her to go along.

104

✏️ ✏️ ✏️ Tantrums Worksheet ✏️ ✏️ ✏️

Does your child have tantrums? When was the last tantrum?

_____

_____

_____

_____

Why did your child have a tantrum?

_____

_____

_____

_____

What did your child do when he or she was having the tantrum?

_____

_____

_____

_____

What did *you* do while your child was having the tantrum?

_____

_____

_____

_____

Were you able to help your child calm down without giving him what he demanded? If not, what will you try next time?

_____

_____

_____

_____

Mindful Moment: Loving Kindness

Handling tantrums can be extremely stressful. In order to successfully help your child through a tantrum, you need to be calm yourself. Mindfulness can be a real gift in times like this. The mindfulness exercise for this chapter is a type of meditation. That means you will sit quietly and focus all of your thoughts and attention on one thing. In this case, the thing you will focus on is a set of phrases called "Loving Kindness." Like our previous Mindful Moments, this one is designed to help calm your mind and let go of the worries you sometimes hang onto without even realizing it.

Sit in a chair or on the floor with your hands resting in your lap. Relax. Start with some breathing.

Take a long, slow in-breath through your nose, filling your lungs completely. Hold for a few seconds. Then gradually exhale to a count of seven, emptying your lungs completely.

Let go of any concerns or preoccupations for now. For a few moments, simply imagine the breath moving through your chest.

First you will practice loving kindness on yourself. It is hard to love other people without first loving yourself. Sitting quietly, repeat the following phrases to yourself, slowly and steadily:

> *"May I be happy. May I be well. May I be safe.*
> *May I be peaceful and at ease."*

Now think of your children, your partner, and other members of your family. Slowly repeat phrases of loving kindness toward those people:

> *"May you be happy. May you be well. May you be safe.*
> *May you be peaceful and at ease."*

Now think of someone in your life who has cared deeply for you. Repeat phrases of loving kindness toward that person:

> *"May you be happy. May you be well. May you be safe.*
> *May you be peaceful and at ease."*

Now think of other friends, neighbors, acquaintances, pets, even strangers, anyone you would like to include. Repeat the phrases of loving kindness toward them:

"May you be happy. May you be well. May you be safe. May you be peaceful and at ease."

Finally, think of a person that causes you trouble or pain, someone you have struggled to love, like, or get along with. Use the same phrases, repeating them again and again, toward this person:

"May you be happy. May you be well. May you be safe. May you be peaceful and at ease."

As you move through this exercise, you might find difficult feelings like sadness or anger coming up. Do not judge yourself or the feelings. You might try directing loving kindness toward these feelings also.

"May you be happy. May you be well. May you be safe. May you be peaceful and at ease."

The Loving Kindness meditation is based on work by Gil Fronsdal from his book The Issue at Hand *(Insight Meditation Center).*

Encouraging Your Child

Of all the parenting skills you have, the most powerful is your ability to **encourage** your children. That's because to "en-courage" means to "give **courage**." The great child psychologist Rudolf Dreikurs once said that "children need encouragement like plants need water."

Everybody has problems. People who learn to face their problems and solve them do better. This takes courage. Your child will need to learn not to give up when she has a problem. She will need to learn to do the right thing even when it is hard. She will need courage to say "no" to drugs and other harmful things. She will need courage to make her dreams come true.

We **encourage** our children with helpful words and actions. We hug them. We listen to them. We help them when they need help. We leave them alone when they need quiet time. And when they make a mistake, we do not yell at them. We help them learn to do better.

Sometimes parents say or do things that discourage their children. This takes away courage and makes children feel they are not good enough. Discouraged children "act out" their discouraged feelings. This means they misbehave more. They don't realize they are acting out angry or sad feelings, but they are. Besides, who wants to cooperate with people who say hurtful things to them? All of us—children and parents alike—would rather cooperate with people who encourage us.

Parents are not bad when they discourage their children. Just like children, we all need to learn how to be more encouraging. Instead of putting others down, look for ways to build them up.

When you want to encourage your child you can say things like:

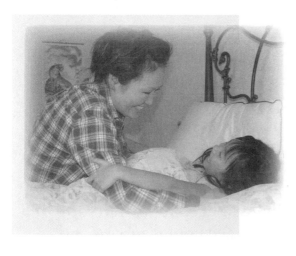

"Nice job."

"I like that!"

"Thanks!"

"You were a great help."

"Wonderful!"

"You looked happy when you did that!"

"You are getting closer and closer. Soon you will be able to do this all by yourself!"

"I bet that felt good!"

"You look proud of yourself!"

Some Ways to Encourage

DON'T PUT 'EM DOWN.	BUILD 'EM UP!
Do not ignore your child.	**Help your child build skills… one step at a time.**

Do not ignore your child.

When your child needs your help, act! Do not say, "I don't have time for you right now. Go play!" This makes him feel frustrated and not important. On the other hand…Do not do everything for him either. This puts him down by making him feel helpless and not capable.

Your child needs courage to learn new things. And he learns when you help him. Take the time to teach him. He will learn to do things himself.

Help your child build skills… one step at a time.

Break big challenges down into small ones. Each time he does something right, he feels good. He gains more courage to try to learn more new things.

For example, you can say, "I think you are big enough to learn to dress yourself. Do you want to learn to put on your shirt or pants?"

"You start putting on your shirt. I will help you if you need it."

He will also learn by doing things himself. He will learn by making mistakes. Let him make mistakes. When he finally does it right, he will feel very proud.

DON'T PUT 'EM DOWN.	BUILD 'EM UP!

Do not expect the worst.

If you think your child is bad, he will act bad. If you think your child will fail, he probably will fail. And if you think your child will misbehave, he probably will misbehave.

For example, four-year-old Doug is running in Grandma's home. He breaks a beautiful glass dish. Doug's mother gets angry and slaps him. She yells, "What did I tell you about running in the house?! I knew this would happen! You are bad news! I wish you were never born!"

Doug's mother was angry because Doug is an active child and forgot about the "no running in the house" rule. He made a mistake. But mother made a bigger mistake. She expected him to fail. And when he did, she hit him and said he was bad. Now he may think that he is bad. If he thinks he is bad, he will act bad. Then she said something that was even worse. She said that she wished he was never born. Words like this are very hurtful to children. They can make a child feel worthless and hateful. They are abusive.

Show confidence in your child.

You are the most important person to your child. He believes everything you tell him. Your words and your actions can help him to grow. If you believe in your child, he will believe in himself. If you think your child is good and smart, kind and helpful, he will act better. You need to teach him to believe in himself.

"Son, this is why we have a rule about not running in the house. Running in Grandma's house was a mistake. What do we do when we make a mistake? We fix it. So, let's get a broom and clean up the broken dish. Then you can apologize to Grandma."

Examples:

"You can do it. You're trying so hard!"."

"Good thinking, Jodi!"

"Yeah! You can dress yourself!"

"It may be hard, but you can do it."

Continued on next page.

DON'T PUT 'EM DOWN.	BUILD 'EM UP!
Do not notice only the mistakes. All children make mistakes. All children misbehave sometimes. If you only take the time to talk to your child when he makes mistakes, he may soon believe that there is more wrong with him than right. He may become so discouraged that he stops trying. He may even make more mistakes to get your attention.	**Catch 'em doing good.** Teach yourself to look at all the good things about your child. Don't just catch him doing something wrong. Make sure you catch him doing lots more right! When was the last time you said, "Thank you" or "Good job" to your child? Tell her what you like about her and how glad you are that she is your daughter. Tell him that you are proud of him, and that you hope he is proud of himself. **Example:** Dad wants three-year-old Jasmine to stay in bed at night after he puts her down. After several nights of getting out of bed many times, Jasmine gets up only one time. The next morning, Dad says, "You got out of bed only one time last night, Jasmine. Good job! So tonight we'll have more time for a longer story."

When you have a child with special needs, you might be tempted to overprotect him. You might think overprotecting your child will make things easier for him. But really you are robbing him of a chance to strengthen his skills and character in the struggle.

Use good judgment to decide when to help your child and when to step back. Let your child feel the joy of solving a problem on his own or with only a little help. Overcoming limitations can be very encouraging!

✎✎ Encouragement Worksheet ✎✎

1. What can you say and do when you are busy and your child needs your help?

_____

_____

_____

_____

2. What things do you do for your child that he could do for himself?

_____

_____

_____

_____

3. What words do you use when you are teaching your child something new?

_____

_____

_____

_____

4. What do you say to your child when you think she will make a mistake?

_____

_____

_____

_____

5. What can you say to your child to encourage her instead?

_____

_____

_____

You need encouragement, too!

You need encouragement just like your child. Think of some good things about you and your child:

I am good at_____

_____

_____

_____

My child is good at_____

_____

_____

_____

People like me because_____

_____

_____

_____

I like my child because_____

_____

_____

_____

I am learning to_____

_____

_____

_____

My child is learning to_____

_____

_____

_____

Where You Can Go for Help

It can be hard being a parent. Earlier we talked about what to do when your baby or young child is crying and won't stop no matter what. What do you do when you are stressed to your limit? One of the tips we gave was to reach out for help. Keep a list of people and organizations that you can call. All parents need help with their children sometimes. There are people in your community that can help you. For example:

- ☐ Your parents
- ☐ Sisters, brothers, grandparents, aunts, uncles
- ☐ Friends
- ☐ A place of worship
- ☐ Your child's pre-school teacher or child-care worker
- ☐ Your child's doctor or children's hospital
- ☐ Books about parenting
- ☐ Web sites about parenting
- ☐ Online forums for parents
- ☐ Other parents

Some of these people and places can tell you about places where you can get help. Some cost very little money, and some are free.

Some parents were not treated very well by their own parents. Maybe they were hurt by someone else. They may be quick to get angry, and when they do get angry they may "lose it." What they lose is control over their actions. They may say hurtful things to their children or even abuse them. We saw an example of this when Doug's mother slapped him and yelled that she wished he had never been born.

Just as children are not "bad" when they misbehave, these parents are not bad either. They are hurt and they need help to get better. They need to learn better ways to manage their anger. They need to learn better skills for parenting their children. If you know a parent like this, please help them get the help they need. This program can help. They may need more help, too.

If you are such a parent, you are already doing something to help yourself and your child. Keep at it. You are worth the effort, and so are your children.

Some places that can help:

Call 911 if you or a child is in danger and need help right away.

National Child Abuse Hotline:1-800-4-A-Child (1-800-422-4453) www.childhelp.org

Parents Anonymous (Find a local group) www.parentsanonymous.org or call the National Parent Hotline: 1-855-4A PARENT (1-855-427-2736)

Anger management groups (look online or ask your doctor)

Local Community Mental Health Center

Can you think of places where you can go for help in your community? Write them below:

_____

_____

_____

_____

_____

_____

_____

_____

_____

_____

114

Home Activities

Check the box beside each activity after you complete it this week:

- ☐ I will practice giving my child a choice and a consequence to handle a problem.

- ☐ I will practice the three ways of encouraging my child and avoid the three ways of discouraging.

- ☐ I will read Chapter 3 and complete the activities.

- ☐ I will practice mindfulness with the "Loving Kindness" activity.

- ☐ I will play "Panda and Frog" with my children (if age-appropriate) to help strengthen their brains.

- ☐ I will use the methods I learned to avoid tantrums and to handle a tantrum if my child has one.

- ☐ I will make a list of people and organizations who can help me if I need it.

Do these seven things at home this week, then answer these questions:

This is what happened when I gave my child a choice and a consequence:

_____

_____

After I practiced encouragement, I felt: _____

_____

This is how my child responded when I encouraged him/her:

_____

After I practiced "Loving Kindness," I felt: _____

_____

This is what happened when I used my new methods to handle tantrums with my child:

_____

_____

CHAPTER 4 Preparing for School Success

Watering Your Child's Beautiful Brain

One of the main ideas in this book is that your child's brain is an amazing thing. It is capable of learning so much so fast, and it is growing every day. "You'll never guess what she did today!" or "Look what he can do now!" are common phrases we hear from Active Parents. They are awed by how quickly their children learn.

To get the best out of that beautiful brain, your child needs love, support, and teaching from you and other caring adults. We said in Chapter 3 that "children need encouragement like plants need water." We want to build them up and not put them down. We want to build on their strengths and encourage them to learn new things. We want to value them for who they are.

Though you might not think of it this way, everything you do to help your young child grow up strong and healthy is getting him ready for success at school. Our job as parents is to help our children survive and thrive in the world in which they will live. Preparing them to do well in school is an important part of that job. Doing well in school is not the only way to have a good life, but it sure helps. It will open many doors that would otherwise be closed to your child.

You are your child's first and perhaps most important teacher. This chapter will help you teach your child the skills and life lessons she will need to do well in school and beyond. We have broken them down into "Six Smart Things" that Active Parents like you can do to help get a young child ready to succeed in school.

What you do during your child's first five years can make a big difference in how well she learns for the rest of her life. So make the time to do some of these things now and you will save a lot of time and prevent a lot of problems later. Plus, you are going to love being your child's first and most important teacher.

And keep it fun! After all, nobody ever said that learning had to be boring.

When your child has special needs, you may have to take extra steps to prepare her for school—and prepare the school for your child. You may need to speak up for her and make sure that she gets everything she needs in order to have the same quality of education as other children. That is called being an advocate for your child. For example, if your child requires a helper, it is your job to talk to the school authorities and make sure they provide this for her. Being an advocate for your child may be a hard job. You may have to work with the school, your child's doctors, and others to get what your child needs. Your child might need to take tests to help the school learn what she needs. But helping your child succeed in school will be worth all that hard work.

6 Smart Things Parents Can Do to Help Their Child Get Ready for School

Smart Thing #1: Encourage play.

The first smart thing is easy to make fun. In fact, we have been stressing it throughout this book. Play is a great way for children to develop their brain connections. Whether they play with their parents, other adults, other kids, or by themselves, play for young children is good for healthy growth and development.

Play with your child. Do not miss out on one of life's greatest joys. Spend time every day playing with your child if you can. Even if you only have five minutes to play on busy days, that can make a huge difference over time. Find out what you and your child like doing together. Experiment. Be creative. Get down on the floor and play. It will help them mature. And it will help you stay young.

118

Follow their lead. Let your child take the lead and make his own choices about play. Follow along with what the child is doing and let him choose the activities and direct the play. It's great to say encouraging things and to describe what your child does (for example, "You want to draw a face? I like that." or "I see, you want me to have the ball.") But do not ask lots of questions or give too many directions. Keep it fun!

Make safe places for them to play alone and with other children. One- and two-year-olds spend a lot of time playing alone. This is how they learn about the world and how things work. At around age 3, they start showing interest in playing with other children. That is why we call it the Pal stage. Playing with other children is a great way for your child to learn about living and working with others. Whether your child is playing alone or with others, your main job is to make sure she is safe. Always keep an eye out for danger. Childproof your home (You can use the Safe Home Checklist on page 54 as a guide.) and double-check play areas for anything that isn't child-friendly. Stay close to where your child is playing so you will hear if there is a problem.

Play fun; play smart. Any kind of play is good for kids, as long as it's safe, appropriate for your child's age, and does not break your family's rules. But some types of play are especially good for kids' brains. We call this "smart play." Remember we first learned about it in Chapter 1, and each chapter in this book has presented a new "smart" game or activity to do with your child (You will learn a new one in this chapter, too.). The Playing to Learn Chart on page 36 will give you some ideas for games and ways to play with your child that will help them learn at each age and stage from birth to five. And here are some more smart play ideas. Which ones will you try with your child?

Smart Play

Here are some examples of Smart Play. If you and your child have other favorite "smart" games or toys, add them on the lines provided.

GAMES

"I spy"

"Who am I?"

20 Questions

Freeze tag

Hide and seek

Hot or cold?

Board games

Computer games

Trivia: about animals, movies, books, or any topic your child enjoys

Imagining: making up stories, jokes, rhymes, songs, playing charades

Math games: counting, sorting, and matching objects, "Which is different?"

My favorite "smart" games:

_____

_____

_____

_____

CREATIVE TOYS

Building: blocks, Legos™, stacking toys

Arts and crafts: drawing and painting, coloring books, clay, Play Dough™, papier mâché

Puzzles: jigsaw puzzles, shape sorting toys, ring-stacking toys

Make-believe: pretend adult items (tools, kitchen tools, phone, etc), tea set, clothes for dress-up

My favorite "smart" toys:

_____

_____

_____

120

Handling Conflicts between Children

Your child's first experiences playing with other children will have ups and downs. Sometimes they will have conflicts. When those happen, here are some things you can do to help:

1. **Put them in the same boat.** When children have a conflict during play, most parents want to find out who started it so they can punish the "guilty" child. This is not as good an idea as it may seem. First, it is hard to know who really started it. Sometimes one child provokes the other child and the other child gets caught reacting. Second, when you blame or punish one child, you teach the other child how to get his friend or sibling into trouble. Then he may try it again in other situations. This is known as "playing the victim."

   A better way is to put both children "in the same boat." This means that they float or sink together. For example, you can say: "Either play without fighting or you will have to play in separate rooms. You decide."

2. **Remind them of the rules (or make a new one).** Many playtime situations will already have rules that you can remind children to follow. If there is no rule that covers your child's conflict, you can make one. Rules let the children know what is OK and what is not OK. If they break the rule, remind them once. Then give them a choice and a consequence. For example, you can say, "The rule is no hitting to solve problems. Either play without hitting or play in separate rooms."

3. **Help them learn to solve the problem.** Let's say the children are arguing over a toy. You can say, "It looks like you are having a problem with this toy. How do you think we can solve it?" Then you can suggest a possible solution. For example, you can say, "When you both want to play with a toy, a good way to solve the problem is to take turns." Maybe you can get them to agree to this and make it a rule. If not, you can put them in the same boat and make a new rule by saying, "Well, you guys can work it out yourselves. But you have to solve the problem without fighting or else I'll take the toy away." Leave it up to the children to take the final step and solve the problem. That is how they will learn. And remember, if they break the rule, you need to follow through with the consequence or they will not take you seriously the next time.

Brain-Building Activity: Working Memory

Memory is a skill. It is something you learn, and you can practice it in order to get better at it. We are going to learn several games you can play with your child to build memory. They will help your child learn to hold information in his mind while working with that information. This is an important skill that we use all the time in everyday life. Practicing this skill will help your child learn language and math. It can also improve his ability to solve problems and think creatively.

These games require only a deck of cards. Regular playing cards are fine, but you can also use large, colorful cards with pictures on them–the kind made especially for children. You can buy these at educational supply stores and some toy stores.

Quick Memory Game

Place one to four cards face-up on a table in front of your child. Allow your child to look at the cards for ten seconds. Then turn the cards face down. Ask your child to use her memory to recall what was on the cards.

AGE GUIDELINES: This game is appropriate for children age two and older. For younger children, lay down fewer cards, and use picture cards for best results. Start with just one card. With regular practice, memory power can improve quickly. Add more cards to increase the challenge.

Matching Game

There are many ways to play a matching game with cards. If you are using regular playing cards, you can choose to match suits, numbers, or colors. You can make your own set of cards with colorful pictures on them, or you can buy a set.

Lay out four to twenty cards face-down in a grid. Always use an even number of cards, and make sure each card has a match. The goal is to pick two matching cards. Each player takes a turn flipping over two cards. If they match, the player removes the cards and puts them in her

122

pile, and then she gets to take another turn. If the cards do not match, the player flips them back over and the other player gets to take a turn.

AGE GUIDELINES: This game is appropriate for children age two and older. Start the youngest children with only four cards and make sure the cards have clear pictures on them that the child can easily name. Increase the number of cards as your child's memory improves.

Sorting Game

There are many ways to play a sorting game with cards, too. If you are using regular playing cards, you can ask your child to sort them by suit, number, or color. For example, you can say, "Sort the cards into four piles: hearts, diamonds, spades, and clubs."

AGE GUIDELINES: This game is appropriate for children age two and older. Start the youngest children sorting by color. Around age four, you may want to introduce the idea of ordering the cards by number.

Smart Thing #2: Encourage learning.

Did you know that it is natural for humans to want to learn? It is one of the reasons that we have survived on this planet. The second "Smart Thing" that you can do for your child to get her ready for school is to encourage her natural desire to learn. The best tool you have to do this is encouragement. Here are some ways to do this:

- **Set a good example.** When you show your child that you think learning is important, you are also encouraging them to think learning is important. For example, taking this course or even just reading this book shows that you value learning! Let your child see that you want to keep learning and keep improving yourself. Your child will catch on. Other ways you can set a good example are to read good books and use the Internet, television, and other media to learn and discover (and not just for fun). Show your child how you do it.

For example, you can say., "If we want to make a good snack for your class, we need to find a good recipe. Let's look for one online like this…"

Or you can say, "Uncle Larry is spending the summer in Puerto Rico. Let's see where that is on the map…"

- **Take trips to fun but educational places.** Kids learn best by touching and doing. Look for children's museums that have "hands on" exhibits. Trips to zoos (including petting zoos) and aquariums are also great. When you are there, point out   interesting things you see. Read the names of the animals to your child. Show interest in what you are learning. And on the way home, talk about what you saw. You can even play a game to help your child remember what she saw and make it more fun. For example:

Parent:	"Who am I? I'm sweet looking. I'm soft to touch. I make a sound like baaaa."
Child:	"A sheep!"
Parent:	"Right! I'm a sheep. Baaa! Like the one we saw at the petting zoo."

- **Encourage your child to ask questions.** Children are naturally curious. They have lots of questions. Do not discourage your child from asking questions. In fact, encourage her to ask more! When your child asks a question, respond positively. For example:

124

Child:	"Why is the sun hot?"
Parent.	"That's a good question. I guess it is hot so we can stay warm enough to live and grow things. Why do you think?"
Child:	"So we can go swimming!"
Parent:	"I like that! A hot sun warms the water. Maybe we can go swimming this afternoon."

You don't have to be an expert or give a scientific answer to every question. Just keep it positive and show interest. Help your child learn how things work at home and in the bigger world. As your child gets older you can help her look up answers to her questions on the Internet.

- **Find ways to make learning fun.** Look for other creative ways for your child to think and learn. You can get the whole family involved. For example, take a hike together. Ask your children to find the most unusual thing they can along the way. Take turns sharing what you see.

- **Play games together.** Board games are still a great way to encourage thinking. A lot of video games are both fun and educational, too. Just be sure that the game is appropriate for your child's age.

- **Compliment your child on how she uses her mind.** Instead of telling your child over and over, "You're so smart," tell her how well she is doing with a specific task or skill. For example:

"I like how you are stacking the blocks. That's very interesting."

"I see you drew a purple cow. Very creative!"

Instead of telling your child over and over, "You're so pretty (or handsome)," say, "Look what you can do!"

125

If your child has difficulty learning, you may be tempted to take over for him when he has trouble. Or you may get frustrated with him and want to give up trying. Resist both of these temptations. Instead, find out what your child can do and focus on that. Work on your patience.

How do you learn what your child can do? You can ask professionals, such as your child's doctor. You can ask experts on your child's special needs. You can do research online. And you can use your own judgment. You might try a support group for people who have children with the same special needs as yours. The key is to learn how your child learns best.

Smart Thing #3:
Read and talk with your child.

Reading may be the most important skill your child will ever learn. Even so, do not worry about teaching your young child to read yet. There will be plenty of time for your child to learn to read later on when he begins school. In fact, it is probably better for your child NOT to learn to read until his brain has had more time to develop. Between birth and age five, children's brains have more important work to do.

There are a lot of things you can do right now to help your child get ready to learn to read. One of the best is to read to him early and often. Even at seven months, a fetus in the womb can learn to recognize his parent's voice and be calmed by it. During a baby's first year, reading aloud to him can help him learn the sounds that will lead to language. The colors, textures, and sounds in books also help a baby's brain grow.

As your child gets older, he will start understanding some of what you read. He will begin to connect the pictures to your

126

words. You can help by showing him the words as you say them, but don't worry if he doesn't "get it." Just keep reading and keep having fun with it. Here are some ideas for how to get the most out of reading to your child.

Tips for Reading to Your Young Child

- **Get your child actively involved.** Sometimes it's good to just let your child curl up in your lap while you read to him. But other times it will be better to get him actively involved. For example:

  - ☑ Get sturdy books to read to babies. Then let them turn the pages.

  - ☑ Let toddlers finish favorite phrases and rhymes.

  - ☑ Ask questions about the story, like "Why do you think he did that?" "What would you do?" "Do you think that will work?"

  - ☑ When you read from a picture book, ask your child to point to what is happening in the story. You can say, "Can you show me the turtle in the story?" "What is he doing right here?"

  - ☑ Point to words as you read. This will help your child get the connection between letters and words. Also point out letters that are in your child's name.

  - ☑ Learn how your child likes to be read to. Some children are more active. Some like to relax and use their imagination more.

- **Pick books that are right for your child's age and interest.** In general, young children do best with picture books. For babies and one-year-olds, try "talk and touch" board books that won't tear when handled roughly. Two- to four-year-olds can handle more advanced storybooks as well as alphabet and counting books. Learn the kinds of books your child likes. Ask a librarian for suggestions. Or look for recommendations by age group at book stores and online sellers.

- **Get cozy.** Both you and your child will get more out of story time if you think of it as a time not only to read together but also to snuggle up together. Remember, loving touch helps calm children (and parents, too!). It strengthens your bond and builds trust. And your child will develop a good feeling about reading itself.

- **Involve the whole family.** Encourage everyone in the family to read. Make sure your child sees reading and writing used in your home for a variety of purposes, from grocery lists on the fridge door to news articles on the computer screen. Every example shows him that reading and writing are an important, fun part of life.

- **Make reading fun!** Act out the stories as you read, complete with sound effects and a different voice for each character. Laugh at the silly stuff. Have fun with it!

- **Make up your own stories. Or tell true stories.** You don't have to read from a book to give your child a great story time. Telling your own stories shows your child more ways to use words. It can be a way to teach him new things or just be creative. As your child gets older you can make up stories together by taking turns adding what happens next.

Talk to your child.

It is not just reading that is important, but also talking with your child. The more words your child hears, the more connections she will make in her brain. This will help her learn words and how to put them together. It will help her do well in school when she is older. So talk to your child even when she is too young to understand or respond. With a baby, you can describe feeding, changing her diaper, or anything else you do with or around her. With an older child, you can talk about things at the grocery store, what you see on a walk, or your plans for the day.

Once your child begins to speak, you will have many more options for talking with her. You can respond to what she says and ask her questions. The way you respond to her will either encourage or discourage her from sharing. So, be encouraging! Here are some tips to help you make the most of talking with your child:

- ☑ Listen with your eyes as well as your ears. Look at your child when she is talking.

- ☑ Show that you are paying attention. Smile, nod, and laugh.

- ☑ Encourage her to keep talking by saying things like, "I see." "That's interesting." "I never thought of that!"

- ☑ Show that you get what she is saying by repeating it in your own words.

- ☑ Ask follow-up questions.

- ☑ Sometimes you can follow your child's lead in a conversation. Let her talk and see where it goes. Other times you can lead the conversation and see if she follows.

- ☑ Always be positive and show interest in what your child says. That is encouraging!

Smart Thing #4: Limit screen time.

Ever since the invention of television, parents have been wondering what to do about it. Is it good for children or bad for them? The answer is that it depends on what they are watching and how much of it they watch. The same can be said for all of the screens available to children today, like computers, smart phones, tablets, and other devices. So it is important that you limit your child's screen time and monitor what your child is watching and playing. Here are some ideas to keep in mind:

Screens can be habit forming. Why is too much screen time a problem if your child is watching healthy, high-quality programming? It is very easy for a child (or an adult!) to fall in love with their screens. But too much time spent watching and playing on screens means too little time is left for more important things like physical exercise, social activity (playing with others), sleeping, creative play, and smart play.

So be careful not to let your child's screens become their babysitters. Make sure your own screen habits don't keep you from spending quality time playing with and caring for your child.

How much screen time should children get? The American Academy of Pediatrics has some useful guidelines:

Screen Time Recommendations

Under 18 months:	No screen time other than video chatting
18 to 24 months:	Avoid letting children use media by themselves. Choose high-quality programming and apps, and always watch or play with your children. This is how toddlers learn best.
2 years and older:	No more than one hour of high-quality programming per day

130

- Watch and play with your children as often as possible.

- Find other activities for them to do that are healthy for the body and mind: reading, talking, playing outside

- Always know what your kids are watching to make sure it is age-appropriate and not too violent.

Note: Media and technology change quickly. Sometimes guidelines change, too. So it is a good idea to check every once in a while to make sure you are up to date. Go to the American Academy of Pediatrics web site (www.healthychildren.org) *for the latest information about screen time for children.*

Be in control of what your child is watching and playing. There is lot of good programming out there for kids to watch or play. Some of it can even help prepare them for school by teaching them the letters and numbers. Or it can help you teach them good values like taking turns, honesty, and being a friend. Make sure that you pick movies, TV shows, games and other programming that is good for kids. And keep your child away from content that is too violent, sexual, or teaches them negative values. To do this you need to watch a lot of what your child is watching.

Children are easily upset by violence. Even if they seem OK, they may have nightmares later on. Be careful not to take a young child to a movie meant for older kids or adults, even if you think he's too young to understand what is on the screen. Wait until you put your child to bed before you watch TV shows with violent or sexual content.

Use rating guides to help you choose wisely. You might not allow your child to watch PG-rated movies at all until she is older. But if you do, remember that "PG" means "Parental Guidance." Do not let your child watch a PG movie alone. Watch the movie with him. Talk with him about mature content and anything that upsets or confuses him. For example, you can say, "The violence in movies is not real. It's make-believe. The horse did not really get hurt."

Do not let your child use the Internet in his own room. You want to be able to see what he is watching and doing online. If he is watching something inappropriate, calmly help redirect him to a better option.

Smart Thing #5: Teach social skills.

Surviving and thriving requires a lot of different skills. Some of our most important skills are the ones that help us get along with others—our social skills. These skills are especially important at school, where children of all different temperaments are required to get along together. Kids who start school with some basic social skills have a head start. Some of the most helpful social skills for school are:

- Getting along with other children

- Taking turns

- Following directions

- Saying "goodbye" to parents

- Following routines

- Sticking with difficult tasks

- Considering other people's feelings

- Having positive ways to express their own feelings (rather than hitting, biting, screaming, or other negative behaviors)

Begin teaching your child these skills before she begins school. They will help her get along better with others and do better with school rules and routines. You can use some of the methods you are learning in this book to teach them:

Make rules for your child to follow. For example:

> *"We take turns riding the tricycle."*

Make a When-Then rule. For example:

> *"When you put the blocks away, then we can read a story."*

Give a choice and a consequence. For example:

*"Either stay next to me while we are shopping
or you can ride in the shopping cart. You decide."*

Use the ACT method. For example:

*"I know you like to paint, but the floor is not for painting on.
Let's clean this up and then we can paint on some paper."*

Encourage your child. For example:

"I know you can do it!"

"You are really good at this."

"I like how you stick with it."

Emotional Intelligence

Social skills are different from academic skills like knowing the alphabet or how to count to twenty. But they are just as important. Social skills have a lot to do with how we handle our emotions. Another term for "how we handle our emotions" is **emotional intelligence.**

Emotional intelligence is a person's ability to:

1. Identify your own emotions and those of others.

2. Manage your own emotions and cheer up or calm down another person.

3. Use emotions in positive ways.

So a child's emotional intelligence is about how well she understands feelings or emotions—not just her own, but also other people's. As your child learns more social skills, she will get better at telling you how she is feeling. She will learn to tell how other people are feeling. She will get smarter about how feelings work.

Babies start out without any of these three skills, but as they grow they pick them up from the people that spend time with them. That's why it's so important for parents to teach their young children social skills and encourage them to learn about feelings. So let's look at the three skills that make up a child's Emotional Intelligence and see how you can help your child learn them.

1. Identify your own emotions and those of others.

We begin doing this when we try to guess what our children are feeling from their faces, tone of voice (or cries) and other clues. The next step is to name that feeling. For example:

"You look sad."

"You sure seem excited."

"That must have hurt."

Noticing how your child feels and naming the feeling will help her learn about her feelings. Plus, when you say it with caring, your child learns that she is cared for and loved. This will give her more confidence to trust her feelings…and to trust you with her feelings. It sets the stage for good communication between the two of you, and it teaches your child how to show caring to others. This is what is called "empathy" and it is at the heart of emotional intelligence

You can expand on this in other ways to teach your child more about emotions. For example, you can name your own feelings:

"I'm so happy to be here with you."

"When you ignore what I'm saying, I feel annoyed."

And you can help your child guess at what others are feeling:

"She must have been very angry."

"Do you think he is sad?"

134

Video Practice: Identifying and Responding to Feelings

This activity is designed for use with the *Active Parenting: First Five Years* video and discussion program. Your group leader will play video examples and ask you to answer the questions after each example.

EXAMPLE #1

Caleb: "I want to go!"

What's a word that describes what Caleb might be feeling?

_____

Use that word in a sentence to show empathy for him.

_____

_____

EXAMPLE #2

Emily: "We went to the zoo and I got to pet all the animals!"

What's a word that describes what Emily might be feeling?

_____

Use that word in a sentence to show empathy for her.

_____

_____

EXAMPLE #3

Baby (Riley) is crying in distress.

What's a word that describes what Riley might be feeling?

_____

Use that word in a sentence to show empathy for him.

_____

_____

2. **Manage your own emotions and cheer up or calm down another person.**

The second skill of emotional intelligence is the ability to manage emotions. Often the first way a child learns to do this is by calming himself when he's upset. You can help your child learn to do this. But remember that to be a good teacher, first you need to calm yourself.

Helping to Soothe an Upset Child

Think about your child and what seems to work to help calm her down when she is angry, sad, frustrated, or feeling some other painful emotion. Try some of the following methods that have worked for other parents and caregivers.

- Hold her gently.

- Talk low and slow. Reassure her with calming words:

   "It's okay."

   "Let's take some deep breaths."

   "Let's count to ten and then talk about it."

- Pick him up and walk; bounce him gently; sing to him.

- Give her a "time out." Create a special, quiet place for her to go for time outs. Do not use time outs as punishment. Use them like they are used in a football game, as a break that will give you and your child a chance to rest and regroup.

- Give him a warm bath. This is especially effective for spirited children. Playing with water can be very relaxing.

- Do the unexpected! Try using humor. Give your child a choice. Use the Act method. Doing something different can change your child's view of things, and that can change her mood.

■ Help him solve the problem… or find an alternative

"Let's calm down. Then we can see what we can do to solve this problem."

"I wish we could_____, but maybe we can_____."

3. **Learn to use emotions in positive ways.**

Feelings help us know how things are going. They tell us if we are OK with the current situation or if we need a change. You can help your child make this connection. You can help her learn to pay attention to the message behind feelings.

One way to use emotions in a positive way is to first understand what you are feeling and then decide whether or not you want to change it. In other words:

**Name the feeling. Then name the change.
(Or keep it the same.)**

You can use this method with your child. For example, you can say:

"You seem frustrated. Would you like me to help, or do you want to do it yourself?"

"You look like you liked that. Want me to do it again?"

"That's frustrating, isn't it? Well, let's see what we can do to make things better."

"I'm feeling very tired. Please play quietly while I lie down for a few minutes, and then we'll read together."

This will get your child thinking about his feelings. It teaches him that he can use his feelings to "check in" with himself and see what may need changing.

You may have noticed that the last example is about the parent's feelings. You can use this method to help your child use his own emotions as well as other people's emotions in positive ways. Both are important for emotional intelligence.

Smart Thing #6:
Stimulate independence.

Learning to do things "all by myself" makes children more capable. That not only gets them ready to succeed in school, but also helps build their courage and self-esteem. Guiding your child on the journey from helpless newborn to independent adult takes a long time for humans—somewhere around 18 to 20 years! So be patient. Don't rush the process. On the other hand, don't hold your child back either.

There are two rules of helping your child become independent:

#1. Do not do on a regular basis what your child can do for herself... or what you can teach her to do for herself. As we said in Chapter 3, do not do everything for your child. Allow her to do things for herself that she is capable of doing.

#2. Help your child learn to do for herself what she is ready to do for herself. Be aware of her age and stage of development. You wouldn't try to teach a one-year-old how to use the potty. That would just frustrate both of you. But if you are still changing diapers for a four-year-old (except maybe for occasional "accidents"), then you have probably been doing something for him that you could have taught him to do for himself between ages two and three.

How can you know what your child is capable of learning? Here are some ways:

- See the Ages and Stages Chart on page 21.

- Look for more information about ages and stages in books, videos, and web sites.

- Ask your child's pediatrician or nurse.

138

- Talk with other parents.

- Remember that every child develops at her own pace. Observe your child. Use your own knowledge and judgment to tell what a child is ready to learn, and when. Don't worry if you miss. You can always back off if it seems they are not yet ready to learn something after all. You can say, "It's okay. We'll try that again later."

Teach your children well.

Because children are natural born learners, they will discover a lot of what they need to know on their own. This is especially true if they are given safe, healthy, and stimulating environments to explore. There are many skills your child will learn without your help. Some of these they will learn better and faster with your help. For example, they will learn to crawl, to stand, and to walk even if you don't help. But they will learn more quickly if you do help. Other skills—like doing chores—will not usually happen without your help. The following are some of the skills most children should learn before going to school:

- Crawl, stand, walk, run

- Zip their coat, fasten their shoes

- Dress themselves

- Do simple chores like setting the table and picking up their toys

- Use the potty, wash their hands, brush their teeth

- Work by themselves on projects like puzzles, making a picture, or playing with blocks

- Know the letters of the alphabet and basic colors

- Count to ten

So, how can you help your child learn these and other basic life skills? There are many good ways to teach. One of the best is a simple four-step method we just call The B.E.S.T. Way.

The B.E.S.T. Way to Teach Skills

B — Break the skill into baby steps.

E — Explain and show how to do it.

S — Stand by to help while the child tries.

T — Tell them what they're doing right.

Here's an example of how it works:

Tania and her four-year-old son, Jamie, are in the kitchen. Tania says:

> *"Just as I promised, I'm going to teach you how to make your favorite flavor of fruit smoothie, since you like them so much. Ready?"*

B — Break the skill into baby steps.

> *"The first step is to get out all the ingredients we'll need: milk, frozen strawberries, bananas, yogurt, honey, and ice. And here's our blender. So now that they are all here, let's go to step two."*

When you break a complex skill or task into baby steps, you create lots of chances for your child to experience success. Each time he completes a step he gets the encouragement that comes from success, and that motivates him to keep going and take the next step.

E — Explain and show how to do it.

"We add the strawberries to the blender one cup at a time and press the button to blend them up. We only add one cup at a time because they are frozen and hard like ice. You can't add too many at a time or else the blender won't be able to cut through them."

Explain and show your child how to do each step as you come to it. Seeing you do it is a great way to learn how to do it himself. Hearing you explain it builds his language skills.

S — Stand by to help while the child tries.

"See which button I pressed? And how I held down the lid? Now you try."

Once you sense that your child is ready to try the step himself, give him a chance. Stand by to make sure he is safe. Help if needed. But do not take over. Just help enough to get the job done safely. It does not need to be perfect–or even close to perfect.

T — Tell them what they're doing right.

This is where the encouragement skills we talked about in Chapter 3 come in. You want to "build them up" (not "put them down"). Build on your child's strengths. Point out what he is doing right. He will feel good about learning something new. He will feel good about you as a teacher.

"That's it! You're doing a great job. We're ready for the bananas!"

Once your child gets a step right, move to the next step and repeat the BEST Way until he can do it **"All by myself!"**

Mindful Moment: Mindful Parenting

For your final Mindful Moment, take a little time to reflect on some memories. Focus on one of your children. Think about positive moments and events from his or her life. Then fill out the chart below in order from #1 to #4.

1. GOOD THINGS ABOUT MY CHILD	2. GOOD THINGS ABOUT MYSELF
3. CHALLENGES I HAVE HAD WITH MY CHILD	**4. WHAT I HAVE LEARNED TO HELP WITH THOSE CHALLENGES**

Your child needs you.

Your child wants to grow up to be happy and healthy. But he needs you to teach him how. The most important person in your child's life is you. The most important family in the world to your child is your family. Whether you're part of a traditional mom and dad family, a stepfamily, a single-parent family, or any other type of family under the rainbow, it's important to show your children that they are part of a family.

Strengthen your family by planning activities to do together. Make your own family traditions. Use phrases like "in our family" and tell your children the special stories of your family's history. Those stories are your roots. They are what makes your family unique in all the world.

Through your family, your children will learn that they belong to a much larger family: the family of humankind. Their contributions to that family will help determine the future for all of us. So your job as a parent may very well be the most important job in the world.

And if you are a caregiver or teacher of someone else's children, please know that your contributions are tremendously important, too. Though you may never see the long-term results of your work, the fact is that you improve the lives of children. That is generosity and success of a kind we rarely see in this world.

Together, parents, caregivers, and teachers help lay the foundation upon which our children will build the future. Thank you.

Final Thoughts

We hope you have learned a lot from this book. Keep learning! Look for more books to read. And if you are taking the *Active Parenting: First Five Years* course, please tell your friends about it.

Always listen to your heart and your child's heart. And remember to keep taking care of yourself, too. Your child needs you to take some time just for you. Do things that are healthy and that make you happy. Then when you do things for your child, you will be at your best.

Your job as a parent or other caregiver is one of the most important jobs in the world. You are smart to take it seriously. And your child is fortunate to have <u>you</u> to take care of her.

Learn life-changing parenting skills online.

Choose the online class that's best for you:

When?
24/7 access during your enrollment period.

Who?
Self-study. Discussion forum is moderated by a certified Active Parenting educator.

What do I get?
After signing up, you will get full access to the class including repeat viewings of the video, admission to the class discussion board, a copy of the Parent's Guide, and a certificate upon successful completion.

It's one of the most important jobs in our lives: raising children. Make it easier with Active Parenting's respected classes, now available online. Each class is filled with video, activities, and opportunities for discussion—just like a "live" class, but from the comfort of home. A certificate is available upon successful completion of the class. Here's how it works:

❶ Login with your private enrollment key.
❷ Watch the entertaining video scenes depicting real-life family situations.
❸ Participate in online activities and discussion.
❹ Read the Parent's Guide and review past lessons as needed.
❺ Successfully complete the class for a certificate.

Learn more about all the Active Parenting Online Groups! Go to www.ActiveParenting.com/APOG to get started.